AYLESBURY TO RUGBY

Vic Mitchell and Keith Smith

MP Middleton Press

Cover pictures:

Front - Woodford Halse No. 4 Box has signalled the 08.15 from Nottingham, which was hauled by class 4MT no. 75035 one day in August 1965, the penultimate year of the route. The locomotive had been "borrowed" from Nuneaton shed. (Colourail)

Back - The Brill Branch was graced by the presence of 4-4-0T no. 41 in August 1935, the line being then worked by London Transport. The train has no continuous brakes, the branch being exempt. (Pamlin Prints)

Published November 2006

ISBN   1 904474 91 8
            978 1 904474 91 3

Design Deborah Esher
Typesetting Barbara Mitchell

Published by
        Middleton Press
        Easebourne Lane
        Midhurst
        West Sussex
        GU29 9AZ
Tel: 01730 813169
Fax: 01730 812601
Email: info@middletonpress.co.uk
www.middletonpress.co.uk

Printed & bound by Biddles Ltd, Kings Lynn

CONTENTS

INDEX

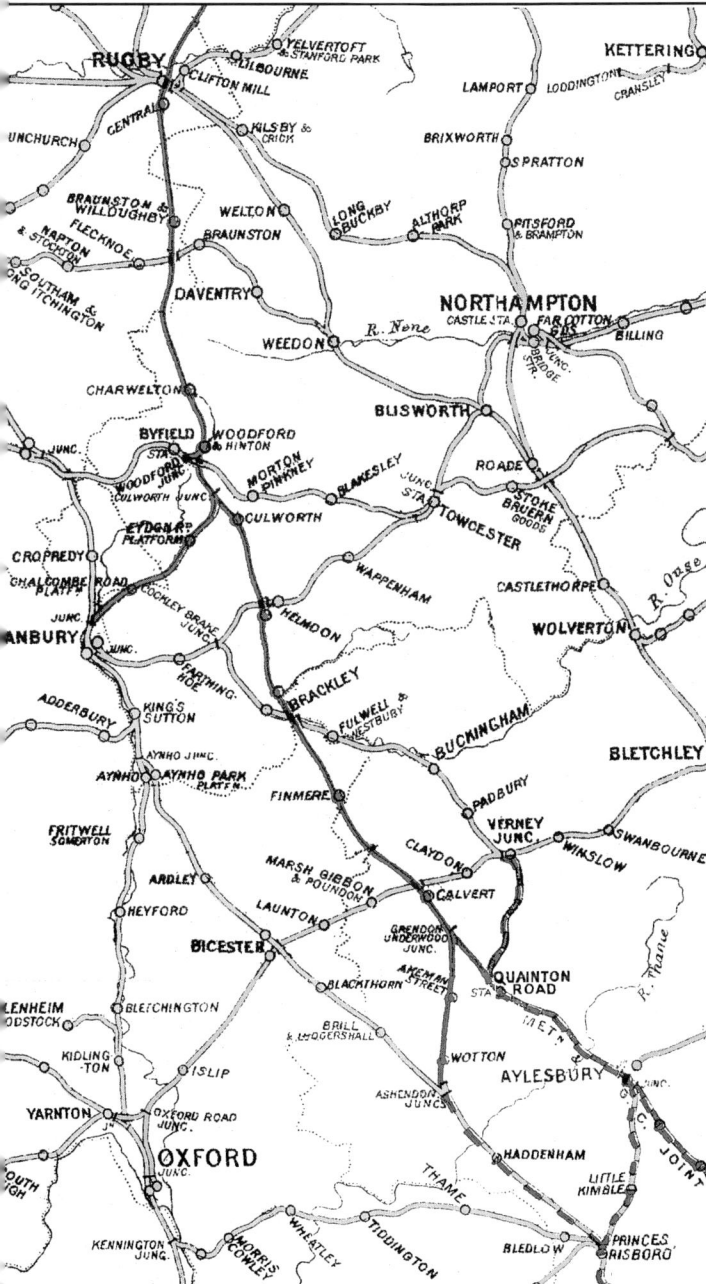

ACKNOWLEDGEMENTS

We are grateful for the assistance received from many of those mentioned in the credits also to P.Chancellor, D.B.Clayton, G.Croughton, A.Gray, R.H.N.Hardy, R.Instone, T.Heavyside, J.B.Horne, M.A.N.Johnston, D.K.Jones, J.Langford, N.Langridge, B.Lewis, Dr J.S.Manners, J.H.Meredith, Mr D. and Dr S.Salter, M.J.Stretton, R.Thompson (Harrow Local History Collection - HLHC), M.Turvey, E.Wilmshurst, D.Wilson and especially our wives, Barbara Mitchell and Janet Smith. Special mention must be made of David Pearce who has been greatly involved in this production.

I. Railway Clearing House map for 1947. The solid line indicates the former GCR route. The Brill branch is shown on the next map.

GEOGRAPHICAL SETTING

The historic market town of Aylesbury is situated about three miles north of the scarp slope of the Chiltern Hills on an outcrop of Portland Beds. The route takes an undulating course over Kimmeridge and Oxford Clays until running onto limestones south of Brackley. The east flowing River Ouse is crossed about two miles before reaching the station.

The line northwards is on the dip slope of the northern extension of the Cotswold Hills and continues on Oolitic Limestone, reaching its summit at Charwelton. A five-mile descent follows over the steep scarp slope down to Braunston and thereafter the route is undulating to Rugby. The small River Leam is crossed on the approach to Braunston.

The journey starts in Buckinghamshire and enters Oxfordshire briefly at Finmere. Most of the remainder of the route was in Northamptonshire, although the final two stations were in Warwickshire.

The maps are to the scale of 25ins to 1 mile, with north at the top, unless otherwise indicated.

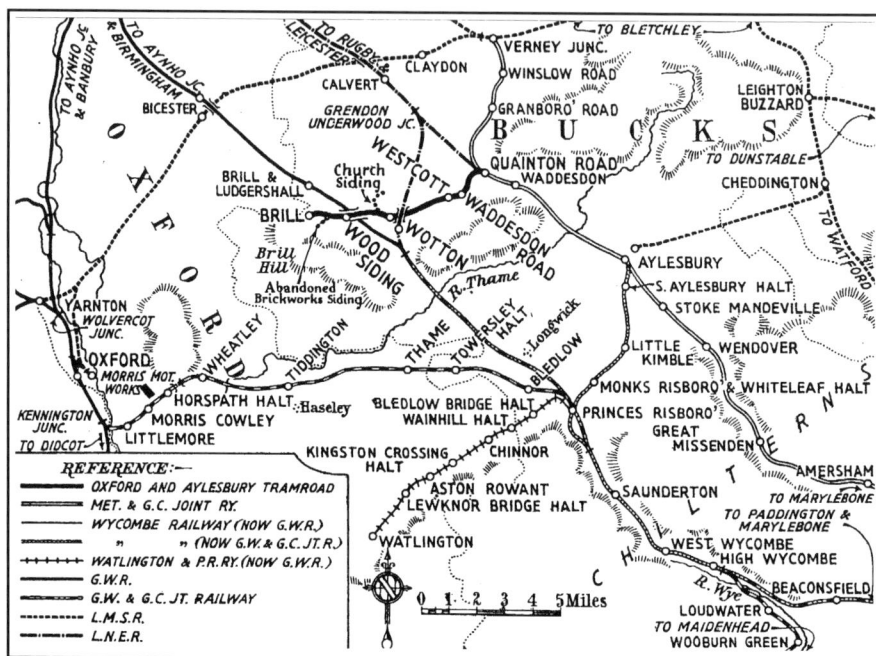

II. The 1930 map shows the Brill branch as leased by the Met.
Brill Brickworks had closed in 1905. (Railway Magazine)

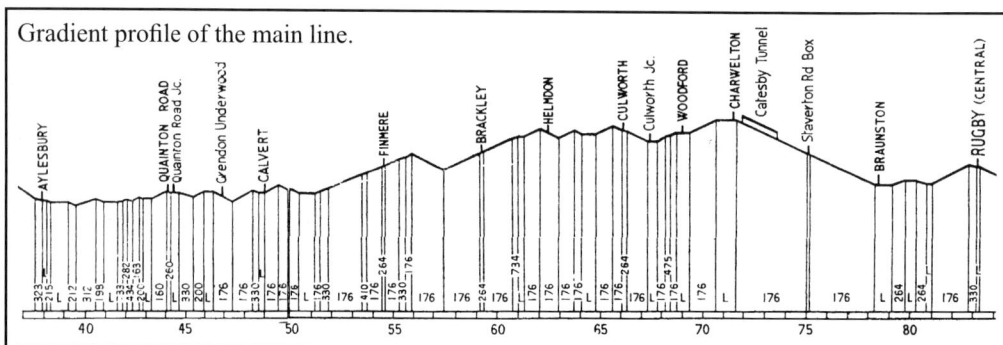

Gradient profile of the main line.

HISTORICAL BACKGROUND

Aylesbury received the first branch line in Britain and that was from the London and Birmingham Railway in 1839. It was for long operated by the London & North Western Railway.

The town's next branch was from Princes Risborough on the Wycombe Railway in 1863; this was broad gauge initially. The operator for over 80 years was the Great Western Railway. This company also worked the Aylesbury & Buckingham Railway's 1868 line to Verney Junction until 1891.

The Metropolitan Railway extended its operation out of London in stages and reached Rickmansworth on 1st September 1887. The next length opened was to Chesham on 8th July 1889 and the Chalfont & Latimer to Aylesbury section followed on 1st September 1892 and trains ran through to Verney Junction.

Meanwhile the Manchester, Sheffield & Lincolnshire Railway had expansionist plans aimed on London and its name was changed to the Great Central Railway in 1897. It made an agreement with the Met to operate over its route south of Quainton Road (which is north of Aylesbury) to a new terminus at Marylebone, the route through Leicester, Rugby and Brackley to London coming into use on 15th March 1899. The Act of Parliament was passed on 28th March 1893.

The plan proved unsatisfactory for the GCR and it made alternative arrangements in Buckinghamshire, by using part of the Great Western Railway's direct route between London and Birmingham. The Ashendon link, between Calvert and Haddenham, came into use on 2nd April 1906 for passengers (20th November 1905 for goods).

The GCR became part of the London & North Eastern Railway in 1923. Upon nationalisation in 1948, the LNER became largely the Eastern Region of British Railways. The route was transferred to the London Midland Region on 1st February 1958 and closed to passengers on 5th September 1966. Freight closure dates are given in the captions, as are those of intermediate stations. The Met came under the control of the London Passenger Transport Board (LT) on 1st July 1933.

Brill Tramway

No Act of Parliament was required for this as it was built by the Duke of Buckingham on his own land and that of consenting neighbours. It was opened to Wotton on 1st April 1871, a further two miles in November 1871 and completed to Brill late in 1872. It appears that passengers were carried from January 1872. The line was reconstructed in 1894, having been leased by the Oxford & Aylesbury Tramroad (OAT). The Metropolitan Railway operated it from 1st December 1899 until London Transport took over in 1933. Closure followed on 1st December 1935, it having been termed a tramway, a tramroad and a branch railway.

Banbury Branch

The GCR built a line southwestwards from Woodford Halse to join the GWR's 1852 main line to Birmingham. Its trains had reached Banbury from the south in 1850. The branch opened in 1900 (goods on 1st June and passengers on 13th August) and had connections with the 1873 East & West Junction Railway, which linked Stratford-on-Avon with Towcester. This became the Stratford-on-Avon & Midland Junction Railway in 1909 and closed to all traffic in 1965. The ex-GCR branch closed on 5th September 1966 in its entirety.

Verney Junction Branch

As stated, this was built by the Aylesbury & Buckingham Railway, but it was the only section it was to complete. Opened on 23rd September 1868, it was operated by the GWR as an extension of its branch from Princes Risborough. It was doubled and taken over by the Metropolitan Railway on 1st July 1891, becoming that company's northern outpost. At Verney Junction it connected with the Oxford to Bletchley line and also the Buckingham-Banbury branch. These were mostly completed in 1850.

London Transport inherited the Met route in 1933 and closed it to passengers on 6th July 1936. Through trains dwindled until closure in 1947 and the track was lifted in 1957.

PASSENGER SERVICES

Down trains running on at least five days per week are considered in this section. Sunday frequencies are shown in brackets.

Aylesbury to Rugby

Expresses calling at both of these places are included. The first timetable listed six trains (3) calling at Aylesbury "when required to take up", plus two stopping trains (2) calling at all stations.

The 1909 timetable no longer gave Aylesbury as a request stop, but offered fast trains to Rugby at 9.40am, 2.43 and 10.55pm (Sundays 5.59pm only). There were stopping trains leaving at 8.4am and 6.17pm, with four others running to Woodford only (2).

Semi-fast trains appeared in the 1921 timetable and so total departures are given hereon: Rugby 3 (1) and Woodford 3 (0). Trains running via High Wycombe increased the numbers north of Calvert.

In 1935, Aylesbury enjoyed departures at (am) 8.4 Leicester (stopping), 9.39 Manchester (express) and (pm) 12.46 to Brackley (4.49 also), 5.53 fast to Nottingham, 7.40 Leicester (stopping) and 8.58 to Woodford. (There were two departures on Sundays).

The first trains were running later by 1950 and the evening service offered a 4.22 to Manchester, 5.49 "South Yorkshireman", 6.18 Woodford and 11.3 to Liverpool. (7 on Sundays).

The frequency at Calvert gives an indication of the local service south of Woodford:

	Weekdays	Sundays
1899	2	2
1920	6	4
1935	5	4
1950	11	5
1961	11	4

From Aylesbury in 1961 there were 5 (2) trains to Nottingham, 3 (3) to Woodford and 1 (1) to Manchester. The final timetable in 1966 offered 5 (1) to Nottingham only.

Brill Tramway

The service was mostly weekdays only, the exception being between about 1903 and 1922, when there were two trips on Sundays, but only one in the initial years of that period. There were two trains per day in 1872-94, three in 1895-99 and four in 1899-1935.

Banbury Branch

The halts were served only by local trains and these numbered three in 1914, six in 1934 and four in 1955. The sample years studied showed no Sunday service. The shuttle service was withdrawn in 1963, although the intermediate stops lasted only until 1956.

Verney Junction Branch

By way of examples of the local service, the number of trains calling at Winslow Road were:

	Weekdays	Sundays
1869	3	0
1892	4	0
1901	7	2
1920	7	0
1935	9	0

July 1882

QUAINTON and BRILL.—Wotton. [Man., R. A. Jones.

Mls		mrn	aft	Mls	Fm. Aylesbry, 151	mrn	aft
—	**Brill** ....dep	6 55	2 50	—	**Quainton**.. dep	9 5	5 45
1½	Wood Siding ...	7 5	3 0	1¼	Waddesdon Road	9 18	5 58
3½	Church Siding ..	7 15	3 10	2	Westcott........	9 25	6 5
4	Wotton	7 23	3 17	2½	Wotton	9 45	6 25
4½	Westcott........	7 45	3 40	3	Church Siding..	9 50	6 30
5¼	Waddesden Road	7 52	3 47	5	Wood Siding....	10 2	6 42
6½	Quainton 151 arr	8 5	4 0	6½	**Brill** ....arr	1015	6 55

February 1890

AYLESBURY and BUCKINGHAM.

Fm Princes Risbro', p. 3	mrn	gov	aft
Aylesbury (G.W.Sta.)d	7 50	1130	3 50
Quainton Road 202 ..	8 5	1145	4 5
Grandborough Road ..	8 15	Sig.	Sig.
Winslow Road	8 20	12 0	4 20
Verney Junc. *(side)* ar	8 25	12 5	4 25
From Banbury, see side	**gov**	**aft**	**aft**
Verney Junc. ....dep	8 35	1248	5 35
Winslow Road	8 38	Sig.	Sig.
Grandborough Road..	8 43	Sig.	5 41
Quainton Road 202 ..	8 54	1 8	5 51
Aylesbury * 199,3 arr	9 8	1 23	6 6

* Nearly a mile to L. & N. W. Station.

WOTTON TRAMWAY.

His Grace the Duke of Buckingham and Chandos, Proprietor.

A TRAIN will leave BRILL STATION for QUAINTON at 6.55 a.m and 2.20 p.m.; and will leave QUAINTON for BRILL about 9.10 a.m. and 6.5 p.m.

THE RUNNING WILL BE AS UNDER:—

		A.M.	P.M.
Leave Brill	at	6 . 55	2 . 20
,, Wood Siding		7 . 9	2 . 33
,, Church Siding		7 . 21	2 . 46
,, Wotton		7 . 31	2 . 55
,, Wescott		7 . 56	3 . 25
,, Waddesdon Road		8 . 20	3 . 40
Arrive at Quainton		8 . 33	3 . 55

		A.M.	P.M.
Leave Quainton	at	9 . 10	6 . 5
,, Waddesdon Road		9 . 33	6 . 26
,, Wescott		9 . 45	6 . 38
,, Wotton		10 . 10	7 . 0
,, Church Siding		10 . 16	7 . 6
,, Wood Siding		10 . 38	7 . 20
Arrive at Brill		10 . 55	7 . 40

These times will be adhered to as far as possible, but the running may be delayed, especially on the return journey, by late arrivals of the Trains at Quainton, or from other causes.

Brill, October 1st, 1887. **R. A. JONES,** *Manager.*

DE FRAINE, PRINTER, "BUCKS HERALD" OFFICE, AYLESBURY.

August 1892

Fares.] **AYLESBURY, QUAINTON ROAD, and VERNEY JUNCTION.**—Metropolitan.

Single 1 cl.	Single 2 cl.	Single 3 cl.	Return 1 cl.	Return 2 cl.	Return 3 cl.	*Fm Princes Risbro', p. 14.*	mrn	mrn	non	aft
						Aylesbury (G.W.Sta.)d	7 50	10 0	12 0	3 50
1 0	0 9	0 6	1 6	1 2	0 9	Quainton Road 237 ..	8 5	1015	1215	4 5
1 7	1 2	0 10	2 5	1 9	1 2	Grandborough Road..	8 15	1025	1225	4 15
1 9	1 4	0 11	2 8	2 0	1 4	Winslow Road........	8 20	1030	1230	4 20
2 0	1 6	1 0	3 0	2 3	1 6	**Verney** Junc. 259 arr.	8 25	1035	1235	4 25

From Banbury, p. 259.	mrn	mrn	aft	aft
Verney Junction.dep.	8 45	1045	1255	5 32
Winslow Road........	8 48	1048	1258	5 35
Grandborough Road..	8 53	1053	1 3	5 39
Quainton Road 237 ..	9 5	11 5	1 15	5 50
Aylesbury * 251,14.a	9 17	1120	1 30	6 5

* Nearly a mile to L. & N. W. Station.

December 1895

QUAINTON and BRILL.—Oxford and Aylesbury.

Fare from Quainton. s. d.		mrn	aft	aft
	Quainton ....dep.	9 20	4 20	6 0
0 1½	Waddesdon **a**.....	9 29	4 28	6 8
0 2	Westcott **a**	9 32	4 31	6 11
0 4	Wotton	9 42	4 41	6 21
0 5½	Wood Siding **a** ..	9 50	4 43	6 28
0 6½	**Brill** ....arr	10 0	4 55	6 35

Fare from Brill. s. d.		mrn	aft	aft
	Brill ....dep.	8 25	3 30	5 5
0 1½	Wood Siding **a**......	8 34	3 38	5 13
0 3	Wotton	8 45	3 48	5 23
0 4½	Westcott **a**	8 55	3 57	5 32
0 5½	Waddesdon **a**	9 0	4 2	5 37
0 6½	Quainton 259....arr	9 8	4 10	5 45

a Stops when required to take up or set down.

June 1922

QUAINTON ROAD and BRILL.—Metropolitan and Great Central.

Miles.	Down.	Week Days only. mrn	aft	aft	aft	aft (Saturdays only)
	Quainton Road.....dep.	9 38	12 5	4 4	6 42	9 20
1¼	Waddesdon	9 48	1215	4 14	6 52	9 30
1¾	Westcott	c	c	c	c	c
3¾	Wotton	10 1	1228	4 27	7 5	9 43
5	Wood Siding	c	c	c	c	c
6¼	Brill ** 76. 80 ......arr.	1010	1237	4 36	7 14	9 52

Miles.	Up.	Week Days only. mrn	mrn	aft	aft	aft (Saturdays only)
	Brill ....dep.	8 20	10 34	3 7	5 40	8 37
1½	Wood Siding	c	c	c	c	c
2½	Wotton	8 34	1046	3 19	5 52	8 49
4½	Westcott	c	c	c	c	c
5	Waddesdon .....[376	8 50	11 0	3 33	6 6	9 3*
6¼	**Quainton Road**.. arr.	8 56	11 6	3 39	6 12	9 9

c Stops when required. ** 2 miles to Brill and Ludgershall (G. W.) Station.

AYLESBURY

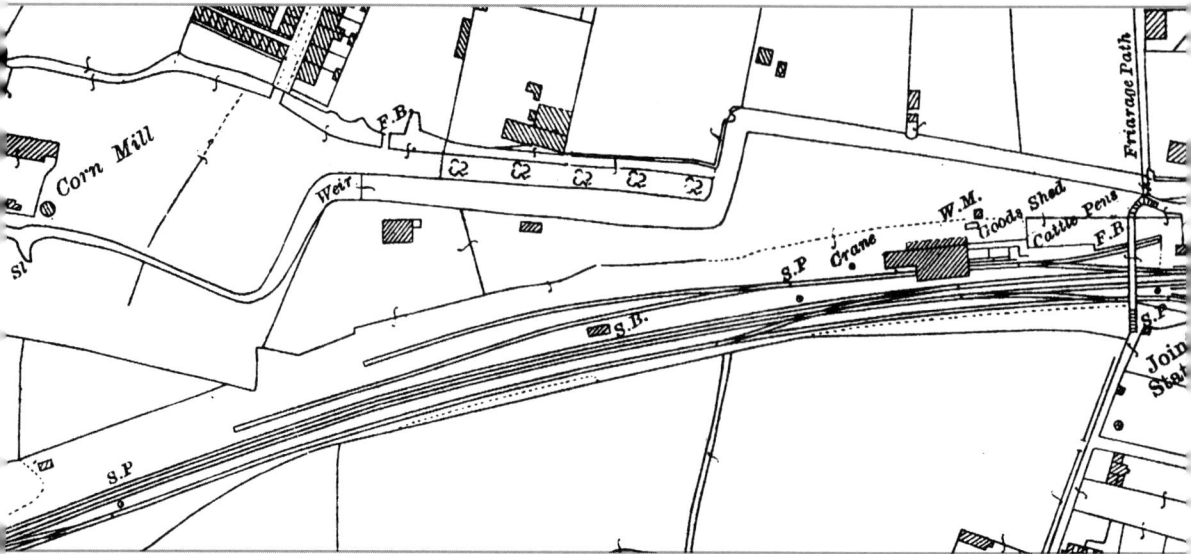

III.   On the right (lower) are the gated sidings of the Aylesbury Borough Council's yard and above it is a GWR siding and its single track from Princes Risborough. Above these are the Met's sidings and main line to London. The map is from 1925; the turntable lasted about another six years.

1.   GCR 2-4-0 no. 24 was recorded with a train from Verney Junction in about 1905. The building seen was completed in 1893; it was rebuilt in 1926-27, when an up bay platform was added. Previously it was run by two committees simultaneously: GW & GC Joint and Met & GC Joint. (Lens of Sutton coll.)

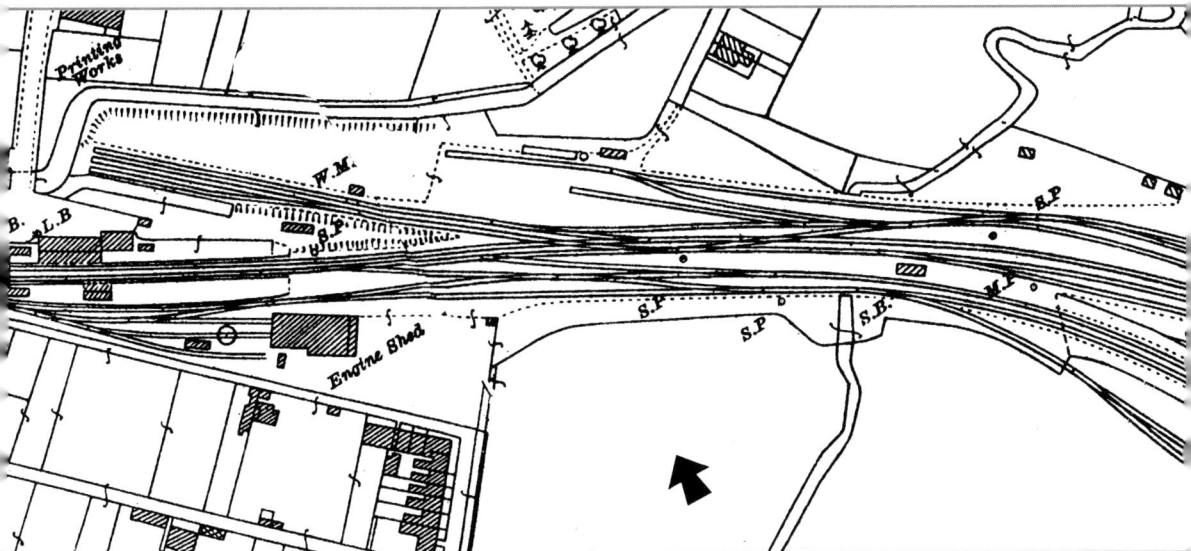

2.	Two Verney Junction trains appear in this view from 8th April 1933. On the left is LNER class J11 no. 5201, while on the right is class F7 2-4-2T no. 8307. The water tank is close to the engine shed, which was in use from 1900 to 1962. Its predecessor initially housed broad gauge engines. (H.C.Casserley)

3.   The 8.20am from Manchester was photographed on 22nd June 1935, the bell tower and extended canopies being evident in the background. No. 6090 was a 4-4-2 of class C4. (H.C.Casserley)

4.   Shortly before withdrawal, a Verney Junction train was recorded on 2nd May 1936. It is headed by H class 4-4-4T no. 107. Met doors had round heads to reduce damage risk when opened in tunnels and under bridge arches. The suffix "Town" was officially in use in 1950-63. (H.C.Casserley)

5.   The map shows two footbridges; this is the public one as BR 2-6-0 no. 76041 brings in a coal train from Woodford Halse on 9th June 1962. Met trains did not run to Aylesbury after 1961. (B.S.Jennings)

**Further details of this station
can be found in our
Branch Lines around Princes Risborough and
Rickmansworth to Aylesbury albums.
The latter includes Aylesbury Brook Street.**

NORTH OF AYLESBURY

6.   Class A3 no. 60102 *Sir Frederick Banbury* accelerates the eleven coaches of the 4.50pm Marylebone to Bradford Exchange on 6th May 1953. The signal box was in use until 10th December 1967. An extensive diesel depot was built on the right and completed in 1991. DMUs ran to Bletchley via Calvert for servicing until that time. (N.W.Sprinks)

2nd Cl   LONDON TRANSPORT   2nd Cl
Issued subject to the Bye-Laws,
Regulations and Conditions of L.T.
Exec. Available for three days   1

HARROW-ON-THE-HILL to
Harrow-on-the-Hill   Harrow-on-the-Hill
RUGBY CENTRAL
Rugby Central   Rugby Central
via Quainton Road
For alternative routes see B.R. book of routes
18/6   18/6

O 1 7 7

Metropolitan & Gt. Cent. Joint Committee.
Issued subject to the Company's
Bye-Laws, Regulations, Bills and Notices.
Quainton Road
QUAINTON RD.   QUAINTON RD
(1)   TO   (1)
AYLESBURY
AYLESBURY   AYLESBURY
10d THIRD CLASS FARE **10d**
Available for three Days

4 8 0 2

7.   Freight traffic was handled in the goods yard until 2nd December 1974. It is seen on 1st May 1965, as the 8.15am Nottingham to Marylebone runs near the goods shed behind 4-6-0 no. 45331, a class 5 of LMS origin. (R.M.Casserley)

8.   Ex-Met 0-4-4T no. L48 is at the extremity of the goods yard on 23rd May 1954, as it approaches the station with the *Railway World* special from Quainton Road to Baker Street. Charrington Redland later had a coal concentration depot on the right. (N.W.Sprinks)

WADDESDON

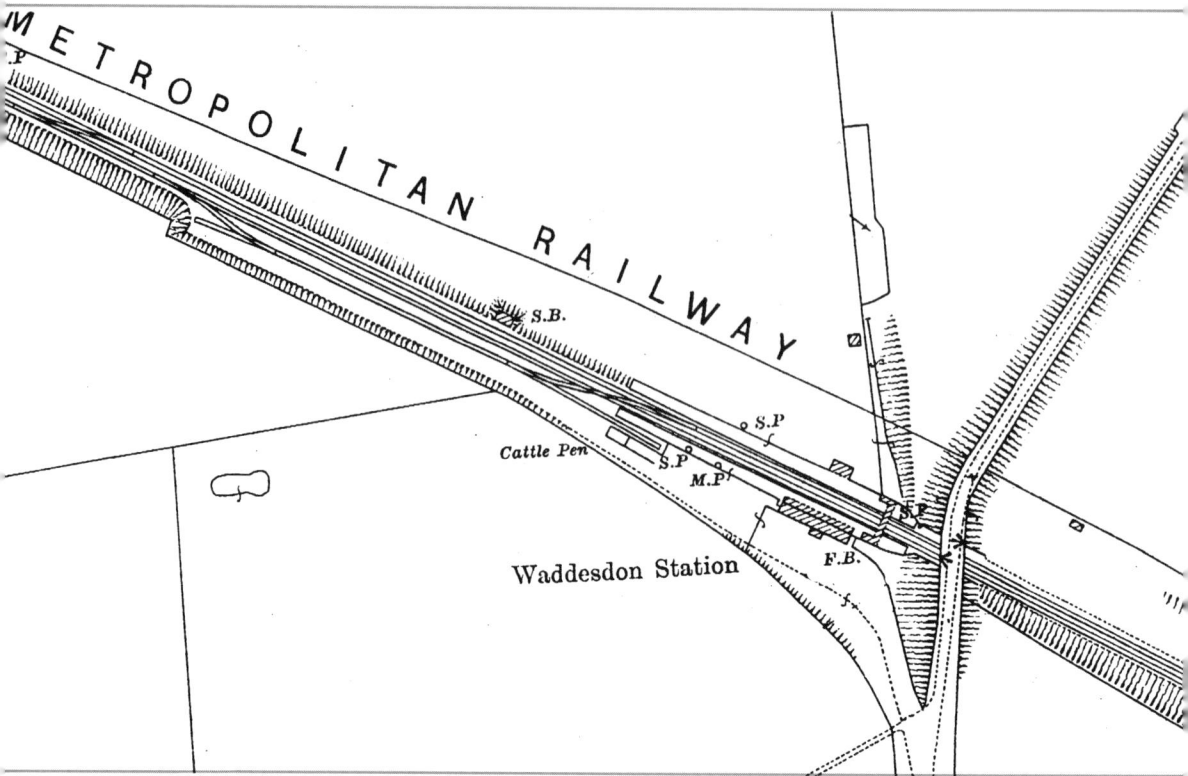

IV.   The station was opened on 1st January 1897 by the Met/GC Joint Committee. The map is from 1925.

9.   The suffix MANOR was dropped on 1st October 1922; there had been another station for Waddesdon nearby, on the Brill branch. A southbound GCR express speeds through, behind class 8B 4-4-2 no. 260. (Lens of Sutton coll.)

10.   The main buildings were on the west side of the line. As the station was served mainly by Verney Junction trains, it closed completely when that service was withdrawn on 6th July 1936. (Lens of Sutton coll.)

11.   A southbound goods was photographed in ideal lighting on 13th May 1939, the locomotive being class LNER L2 2-6-4T no. 6161. Aylesbury Vale Parkway station was planned for opening in 2009, on a site one mile south of here. This would become the terminus for some London trains for the benefit of commuters. (H.C.Casserley)

QUAINTON ROAD

V. The 1920 edition has the Brill Tramway lower
left and the line from Aylesbury on the right.

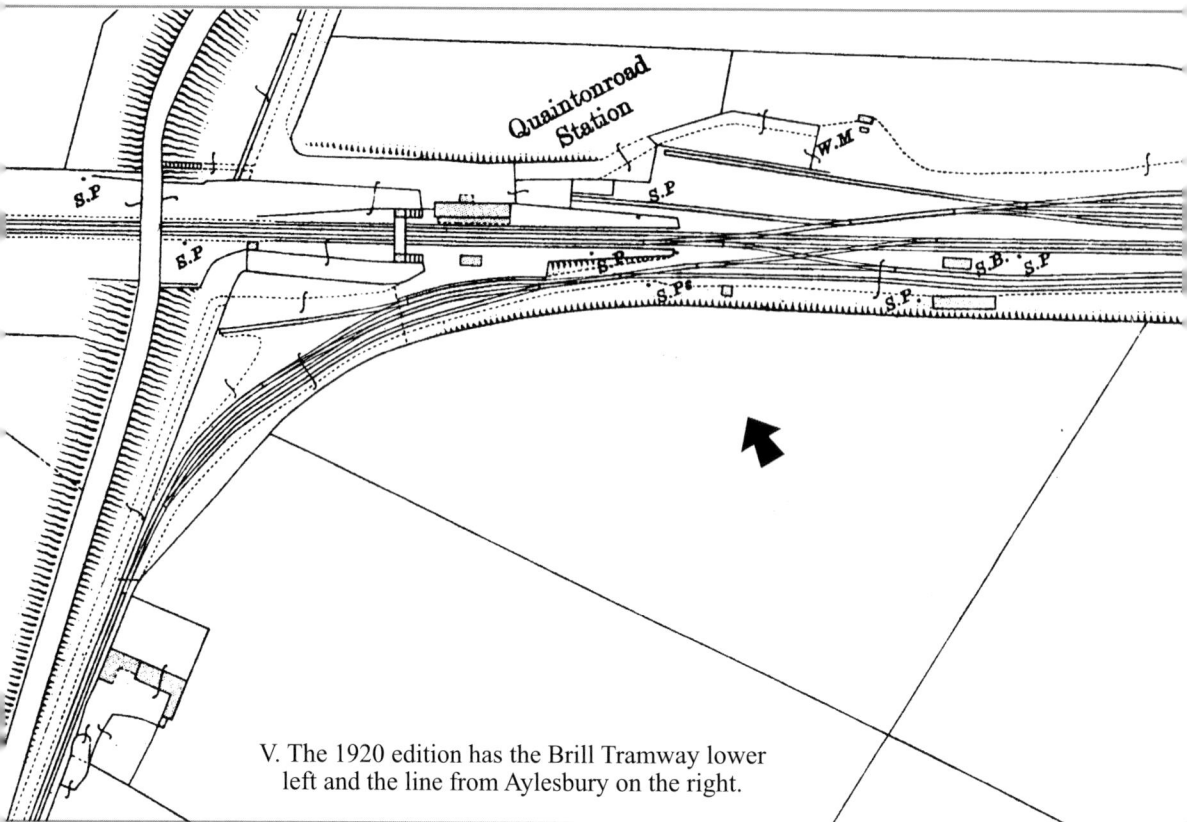

The first station was west of the road and both the railway and the tramway passed over it
on the level. All traffic to and from the latter had to use the 13ft wagon turntable shown.

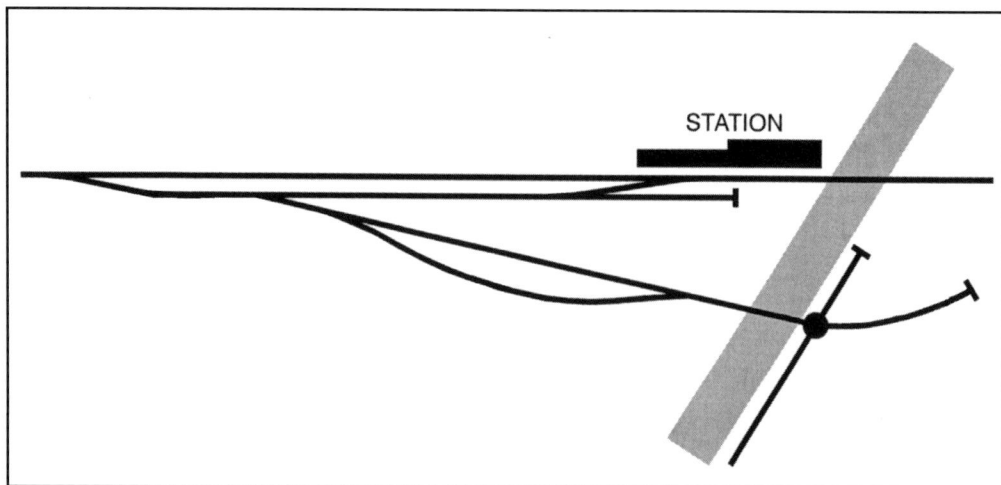

STATION

METROPOLITAN RAILWAY

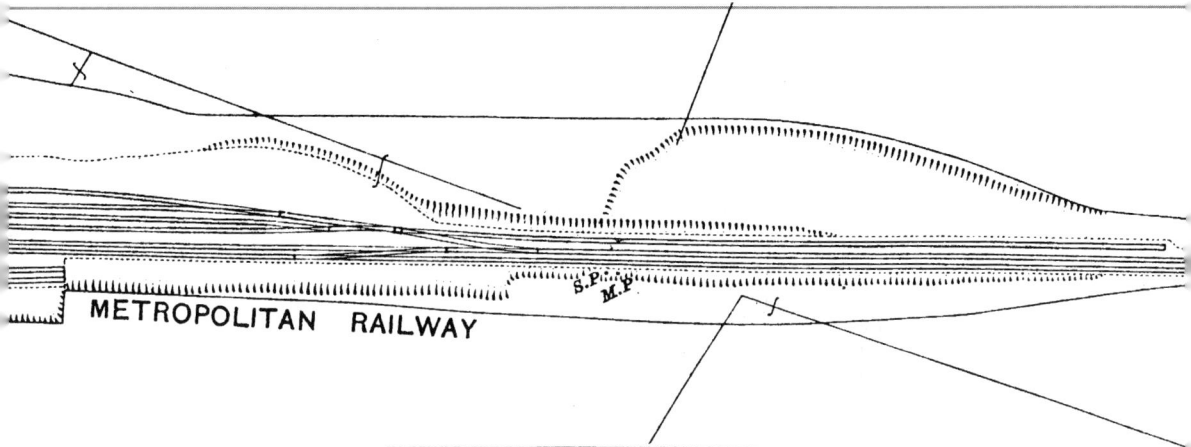

S.P.
M.P.

12.   Quainton Road Junction signal box is indistinct in the distance, as the staff are about to gain fame by appearing on a postcard. The large ventilator is explained by the sign under the canopy. The bridge replaced the level crossing in 1896. (Lens of Sutton coll.)

13.   The junction signals had been moved by the time that the 3.30pm from Verney Junction was pictured on 15th March 1930. It is hauled by class F1 2-4-2T no. 5594. The bridge was designed for quadruple track. (H.C.Casserley)

14.   A view towards Aylesbury on 5th September 1962 has the connection to Brill on the right. The exchange sidings on the left appear to contain wagons awaiting repair or scrap. The signal box was built by the Met & GC and had 55 levers; it closed on 13th August 1967. (SLS)

15.   A Derby-built DMU works the 3.20pm Aylesbury to Brackley Central in extreme cold on 23rd February 1963. Temperatures were below zero for around three months and much needed coal often froze solid in the wagons. The station closed to passengers on 4th March 1963 and to goods on 4th July 1966. (B.S.Jennings)

16.   The Quainton Road Society Ltd was formed in 1969 and the area of the sidings was obtained for restoration work. This is the scene from the footbridge on 12th April 1976. The through line maintained a link with Bletchley. A few Saturday Christmas shopper specials ran between Aylesbury and Bletchley in 1988, calling here. (F.Hornby)

17.   A demonstration line was established and visiting it on 7th May 1990 was ex-GWR "Castle" class 4-6-0 no. 5080 *Defiant*. On the left is a 1952 British-built railcar set repatriated from Egypt in 1985 by the Sentinel Trust. It was constructed to the Berne loading gauge, as was the GCR, which had ambitions of through running to France. The 3-car unit has four articulated bogies, a horizontal marine boiler (which uses ships' bunker fuel oil) and two underfloor horizontal engines. (P.G.Barnes)

18.   The north elevation was restored to its 1900 condition, but with LNER boards. A MR horse-drawn crane was on show on 4th October 1998. It was moved into the museum when this was completed. (P.G.Barnes)

19. Occasionally a shuttle service is operated from Aylesbury for special events and a Turbo DMU of Chiltern Trains was in use on 25th April 1992. The connection was often provided on May and August Bank Holiday Mondays. (P.G.Barnes)

VI. Buckinghamshire Railway Centre in 2006. The buildings on the right had been emergency wartime food stores and converted to a museum and reserve collection store by the Society in 2004.

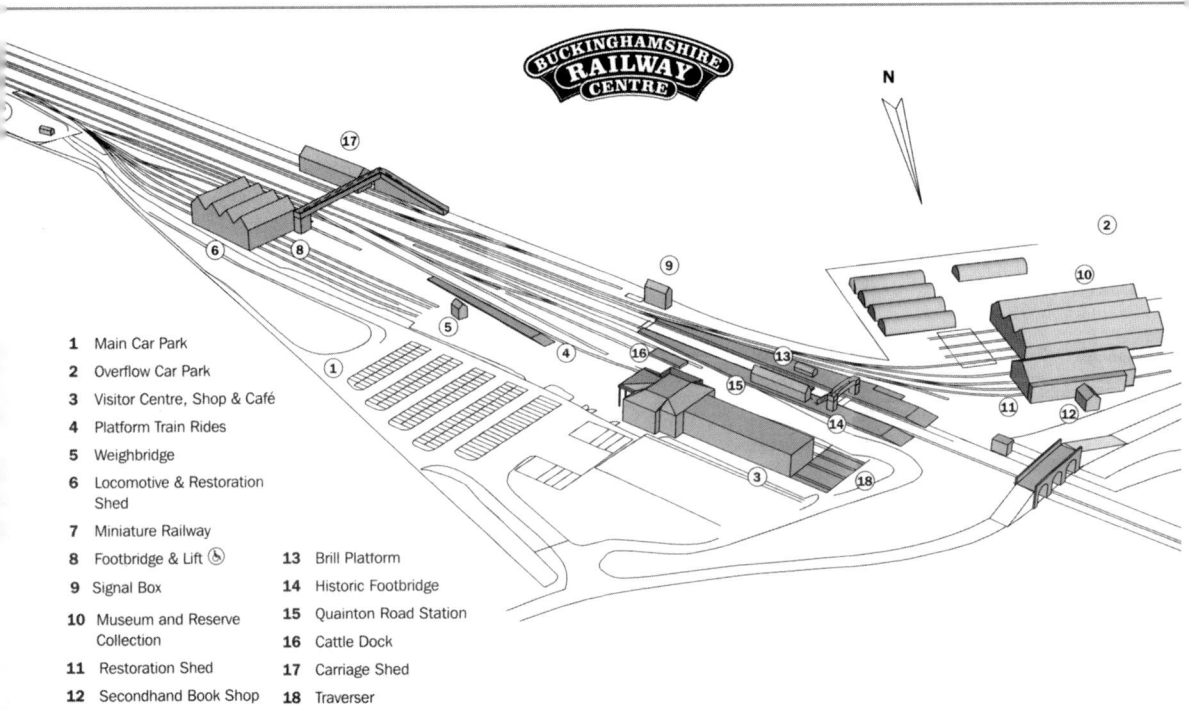

1 Main Car Park
2 Overflow Car Park
3 Visitor Centre, Shop & Café
4 Platform Train Rides
5 Weighbridge
6 Locomotive & Restoration Shed
7 Miniature Railway
8 Footbridge & Lift
9 Signal Box
10 Museum and Reserve Collection
11 Restoration Shed
12 Secondhand Book Shop
13 Brill Platform
14 Historic Footbridge
15 Quainton Road Station
16 Cattle Dock
17 Carriage Shed
18 Traverser

20.   The buildings in the background were erected in around 1896 and the one with the curved roof housed an exhibition about the Brill Tramway. The signal box had been constructed near the site of the original one. Working on 9th October 2005 was Peckett 0-4-0ST no. 2105 of 1948. (P.G.Barnes)

21.   Photographed on the same day was the former LNWR Rewley Road station, which had been transported from Oxford and meticulously rebuilt in 1999-2000. It had been listed Grade II* and can be seen in pictures 1-11 in our *Oxford to Bletchley* album. (P.G.Barnes)

22.   The train shed soon housed many historic exhibits and served visitors in a variety of ways. Ex-GWR "Castle" class no. 5080 *Defiant* was on loan from Tyseley Locomotive Works. To the left is an ex-LNWR dining car. Off the concourse is a spacious refreshment room and a shop of generous proportions. (BRC)

23.   A panorama from the original footbridge on 30th September 2006 includes the wartime stores, a Peckett 0-4-0ST of 1948 (posing as BR no. 2087) and a wide variety of historic stock. The museum (left) houses an outstanding collection of exhibits. On site were ten steam locos which once worked on BR and 18 from industry. (V.Mitchell)

Brill Branch

VII.   An extract from the 1 ins to 1 mile survey of 1926 has Quainton top right and Brill lower left. The branch initially runs parallel to the road to Quainton for one mile, crosses the A41 and a short disused branch is shown running southwards from Westcott station. Another, but longer one, is marked north from Wotton Underwood. This was known as the Kingswood Branch and it served two coal merchants until about 1915. It had not been relaid since the tramway days. A short part at its southern end was retained and known as Church Siding. Ashendon Junction is near the lower border and the two main lines diverge from it. After passing through woods, the branch terminates in a field one mile north of Brill, but over 200ft lower than the village. This had a population of 1206 in 1901. Parcel traffic was handled at the manager's house in the village.

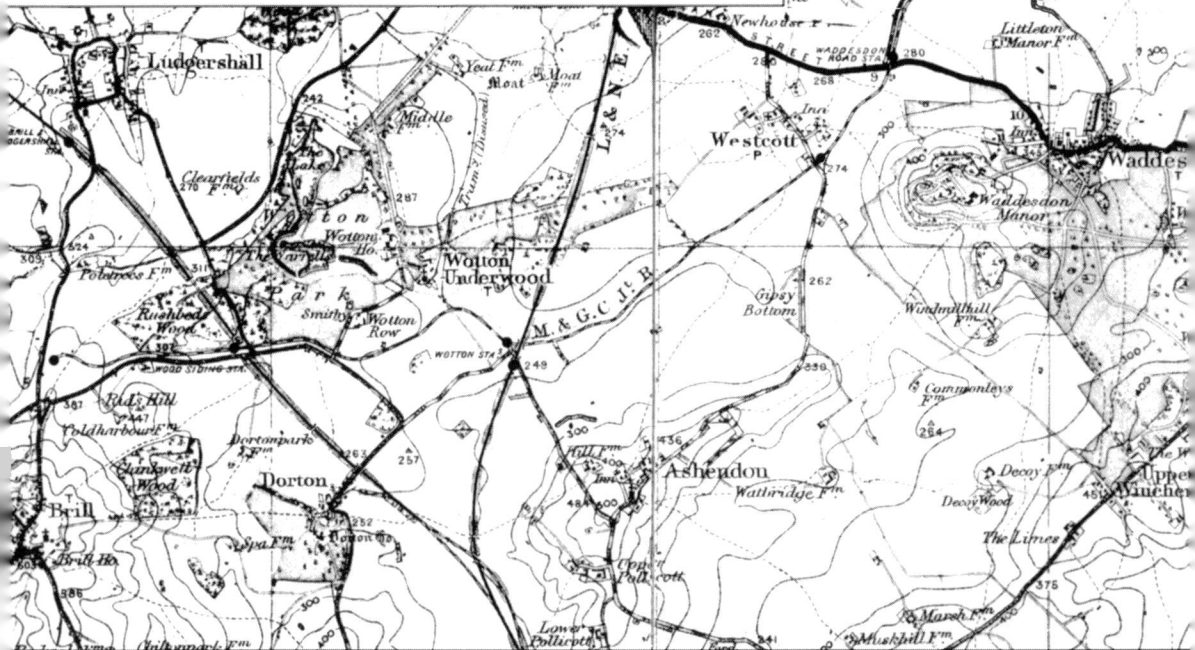

QUAINTON ROAD

24.   Initially, the line was operated by horses and then an Aveling & Porter geared engine of this type was added to the team. A second such engine was purchased late in 1872. They had a chain driving all wheels from a pinion. This view from about 1890 includes limewashed cattle wagons. The pioneer is preserved at London's Transport Museum; its maximum speed was 7mph. (G.Kerley coll./HLHC)

25.   The OAT agreement to work the line was dated 17th July 1888 and electric traction was envisaged, but not implemented. However, the operation did not commence until after a new lease was signed on 22nd November 1894. This is the passenger stock provided. (Lens of Sutton coll.)

26.   The OAT purchased two Manning Wardle saddle tanks secondhand. No. 1 was built in 1876 and is seen here named *Huddersfield*. The other was no. 2 *Brill* of 1894. This view is from the 1894-99 period. The line's first conventional loco had been hired from W.G.Bagnall in January 1877 and was named *Buckingham*. It was returned in March 1878 and replaced by them with *Wotton*, which lasted about 20 years. The leading vehicle was supplied to the Wotton Tramway in 1872; the second was from 1895. (P.Q.Treloar coll.)

2257   MET. & G. JT. COMMITTEE.
Available on day of issue only.
WOTTON (O.&A.T.)
WOTTON(O.&A.T.)   WOTTON (O.&A.T
H   TO   Series 1
AYLESBURY J'NT
AYLESBURY Joint   AYLESBURY Joint
Change at Quainton Road
FARE 10d THIRD CLASS 10d
2257

1556   **OXFORD & AYLESBURY TRAMROAD.**
NOT TRANSFERABLE.
AVAILABLE ON DAY OF ISSUE ONLY
BRILL
BRILL   TO   BRILL
BAKER STREET
BAKER STREET   BAKER STREET
Fare 3/11½   **THIRD CLASS**   Fare 3/11½
1556

27.   No. 1 was replaced by no. 3 *Wotton* of 1899 vintage. It is also seen at Quainton Road at about that time. The track was initially laid with longitudinal timbers, to avoid tripping the horses, but this limited the locomotive weight to nine tons. (F.Moores)

28.   In its final years, the branch was worked by ex-Inner Circle Met 4-4-0Ts nos 23 and 41. This is no. 23 with an ex-Met non-bogie eight-wheeler of 1879. The loco is preserved in London's Transport Museum. (P.Q.Treloar coll.)

29.   The Brill platform at Quainton Road is seen in the 1960s, when it was a very peaceful place. Little had changed in 60 years. The branch had been completely relaid twice: the OAT was able to run at up to 12mph and the Met improvements allowed 25mph. (Lens of Sutton coll.)

WEST OF QUAINTON ROAD

30.   A short distance from Quainton Road was a level crossing close to a cross roads. There were more gates on the road to Winslow, but these were to control cattle and had to be opened by motorists; the train crew was responsible for the ones seen. (C.L.Turner/HLHC)

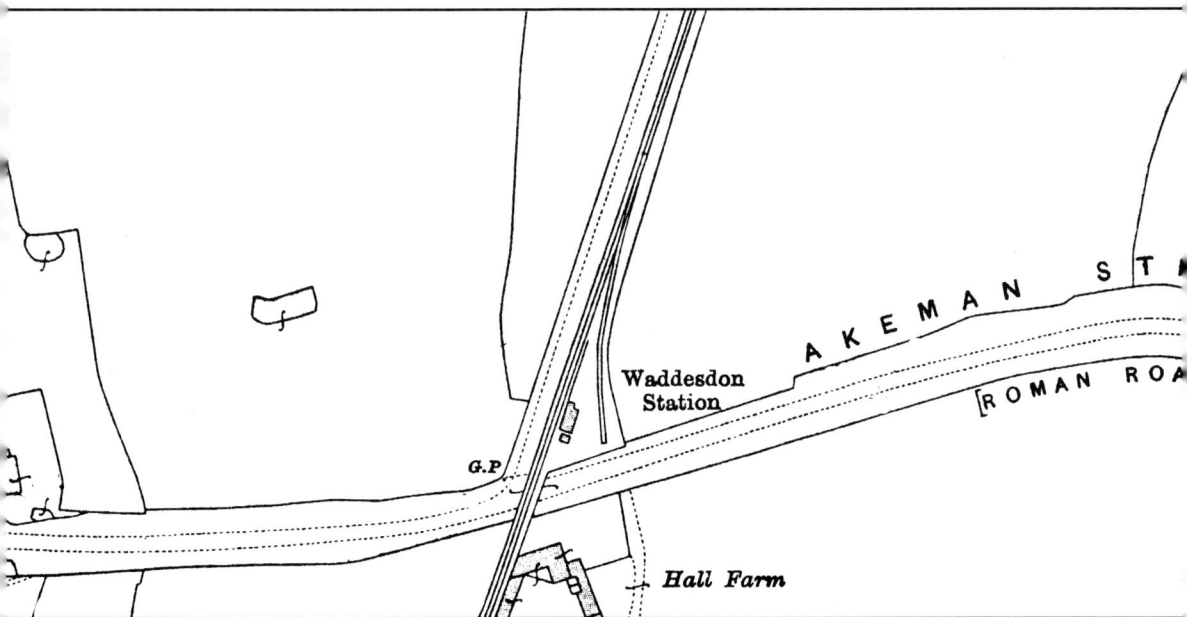

VIII.   The 1920 extract shows the name before the suffix was added on 1st October 1922. Initially it was known as "Waddesdon Road Siding". Akeman Street became the A41 in 1919.

31.   It appears that the initial tramway platform was extended at railway height. This would have facilitated the loading of milk churns in particular. (C.L.Turner/HLHC)

32. We now enjoy two photographs from 8th April 1933. Staffed in the early years, there is evidence of the comforts of a fireplace and a urinal. (H.C.Casserley)

33. No. 23 was Met class A and was built in 1866 by Beyer Peacock. It also appears in picture 28 as well as others later. Wagons ceased to be privately owned during World War II. (H.C.Casserley)

WESTCOTT

☐ *Pump House*

Westcott Farm

Station

C O T T

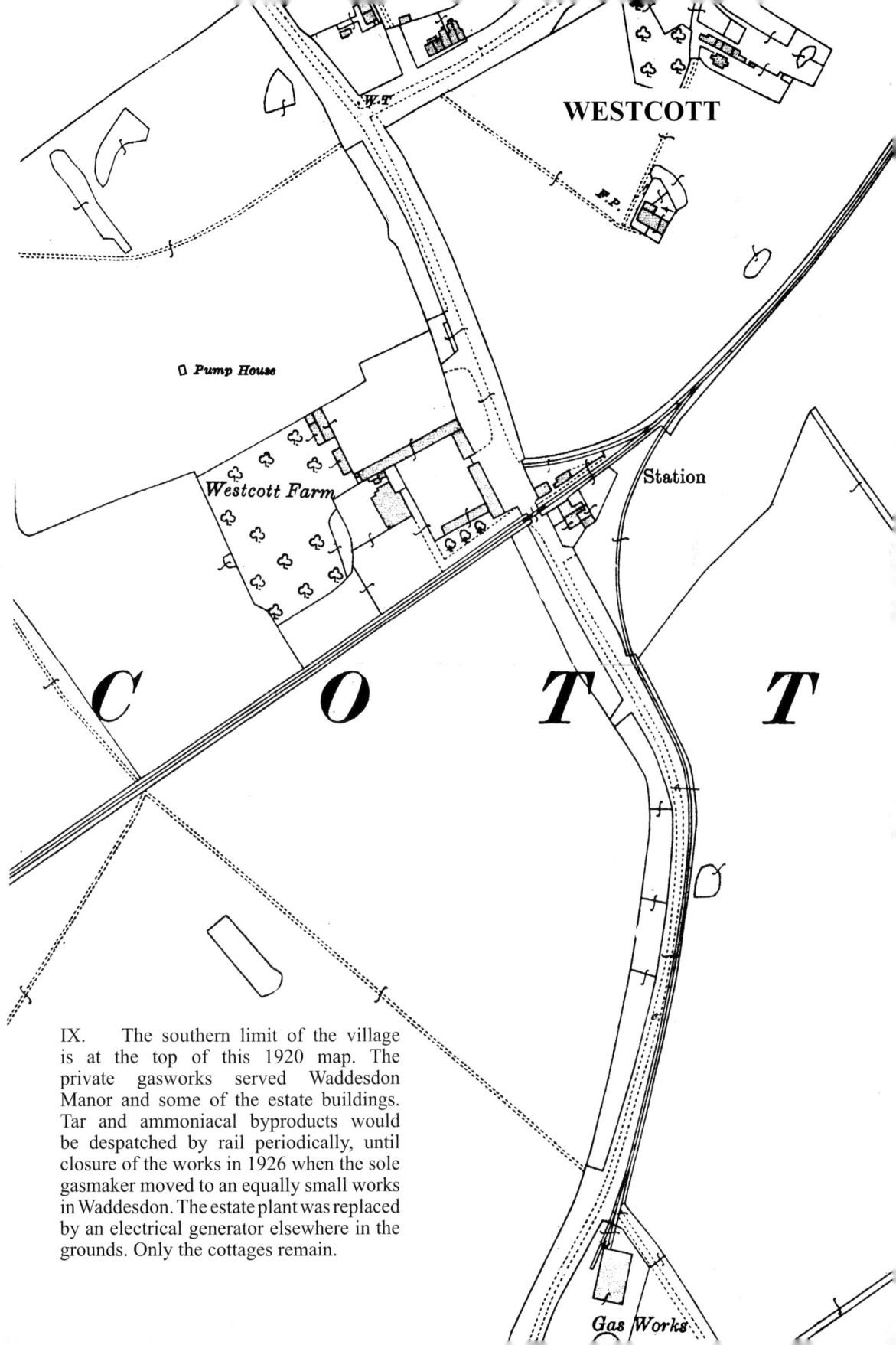

IX.   The southern limit of the village is at the top of this 1920 map. The private gasworks served Waddesdon Manor and some of the estate buildings. Tar and ammoniacal byproducts would be despatched by rail periodically, until closure of the works in 1926 when the sole gasmaker moved to an equally small works in Waddesdon. The estate plant was replaced by an electrical generator elsewhere in the grounds. Only the cottages remain.

Gas Works

34.   The rear of one of the Manning Wardle saddle tanks is featured and so this dates the photograph to within the last few years of the 19th century. (G.Kerley coll./HLHC)

35.   We look towards Quainton Road and see evidence that the station was staffed. The man's responsibility included the level crossing gates and the oil lamps. (C.L.Turner/HLHC)

36.   The single siding is behind the fence in this westward view. The name "Westcott Siding" was applied initially, when the population was about 150. (C.L.Turner/HLHC)

37.   Met 4-4-0T no. 41 waits for the photographer on 27th August 1932. This crossing was over the lane to Ashendon. (F.M.Gates/HLHC)

WOTTON (LT)

Navi

Church
Siding

F.P.

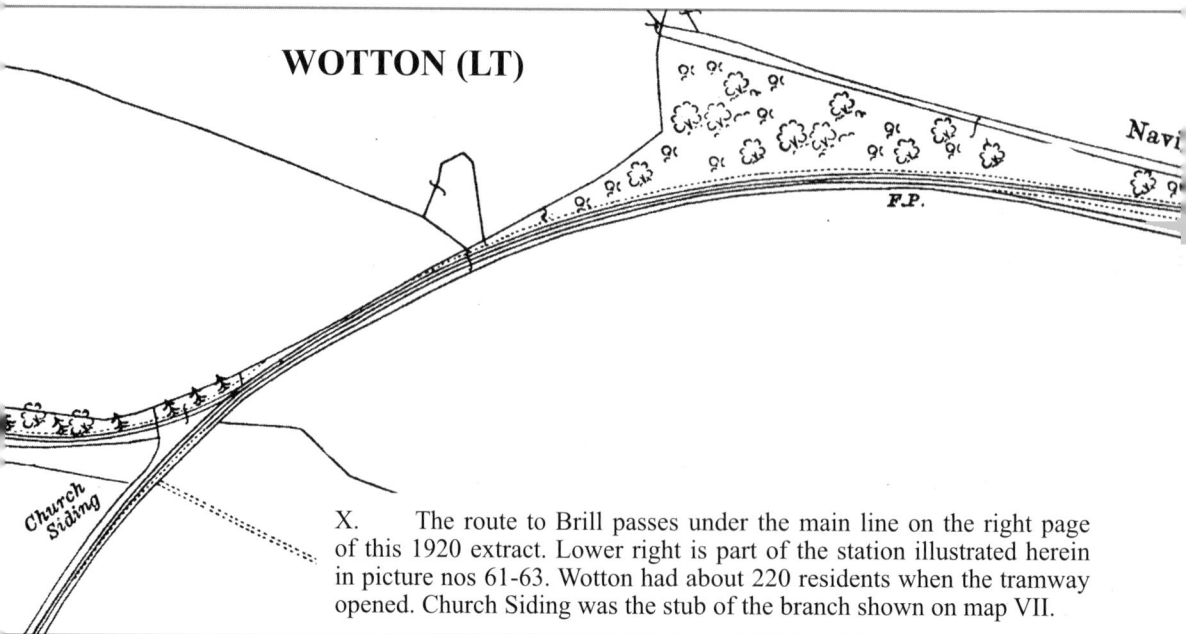

X.　　The route to Brill passes under the main line on the right page of this 1920 extract. Lower right is part of the station illustrated herein in picture nos 61-63. Wotton had about 220 residents when the tramway opened. Church Siding was the stub of the branch shown on map VII.

38.　　The goods shed was unique on the line, but, like the others, had a small floor area. This westward view was recorded during the construction of the 1906 link. The siding on the left did not last. The stables for the tramway horses had been located here. (G.Kerley coll./HLHC)

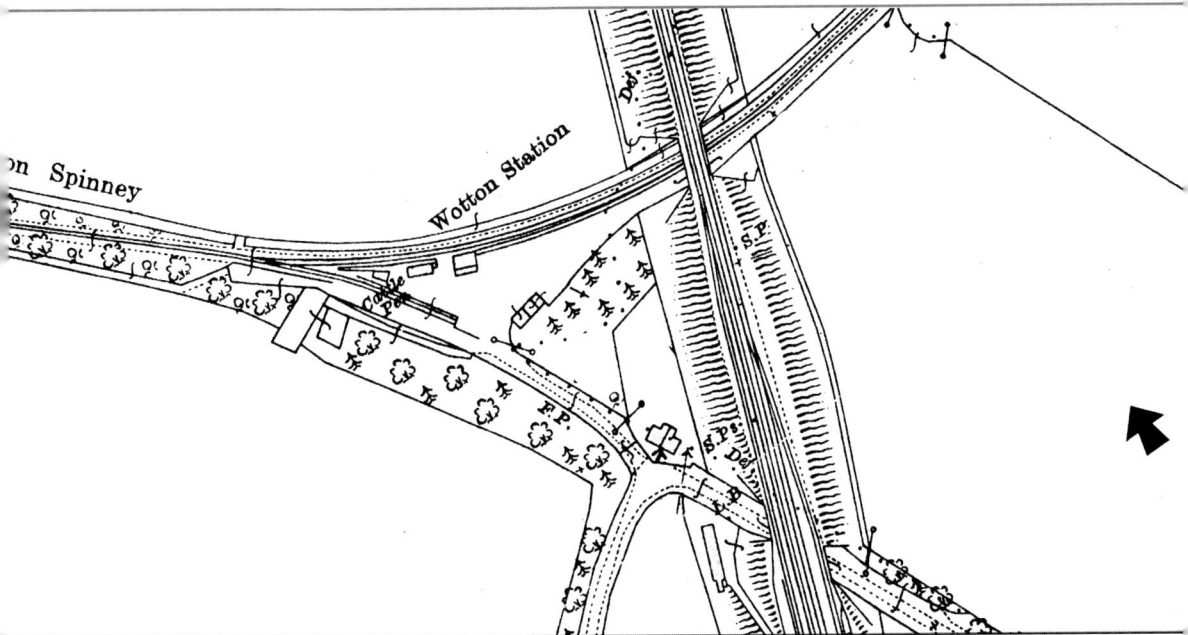

Spinney   Wotton Station

39.   A closer look at the station shows it to have a level platform. There was little habitation for almost a mile. The single line was divided here for operating purposes, with a blue staff eastwards and a red one westwards. (C.L.Turner/HLHC)

40.   Looking in the other direction, we see the second siding and evidence of the cattle pens it once served. Also included is the main line bridge and a sign of staff being present. (C.L.Turner/HLHC)

41.   The 12.50pm from Quainton Road was photographed from the goods shed on 6th May 1935. The unusual cab profile of the A class was due to their late provision; they had none when working in tunnels, their normal habitat in earlier life. (R.S.Carpenter coll.)

WOOD SIDING

42.   This photograph was taken a few minutes after picture 37, the train having just passed over the level crossing on the lane to Ludgershall. On the left is part of the bridge over the main line. (F.M.Gates/HLHC)

Metropolitan & Gt. Cent. Jt. Ctee.
Available on day of issue only.
Issued subject to the Company's
By-Laws, Regulations, Bills and Notices.

Brill

BRILL   BRILL

TO

WOOD SIDING

WOOD SIDING   WOOD SIDING

1½d. THIRD CLASS 1½d.

1173

MET., & G, C, JT. COMMITTEE.
Available on day of issue only.

WADDESDON (O.&A.T.)

WADDESDON (O. &A.T)   WADDESDON (O.&A.T)

H   TO   Series 1

WESTCOTT (O.&A.T.)

WESTCOTT (O.&A.T.)   WESTCOTT (O.&A.T)

FARE 1d THIRD CLASS 1d

010/010

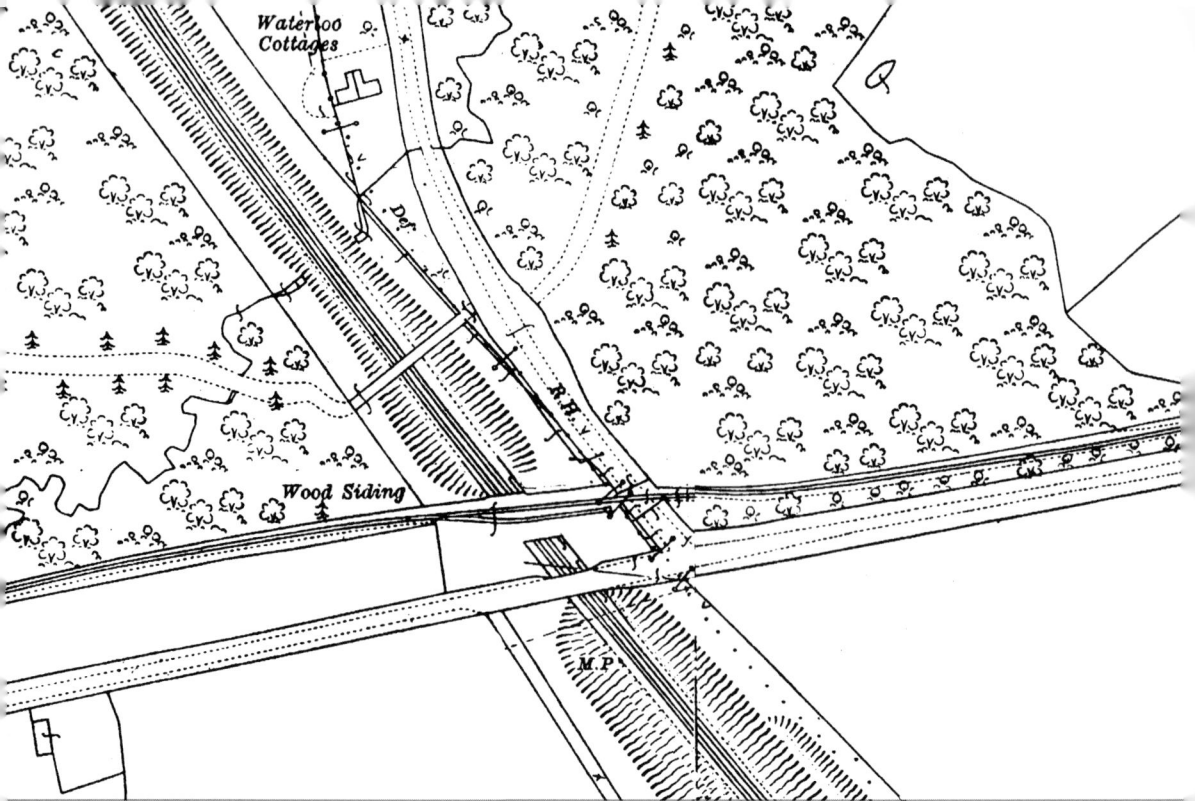

XI.   The Brill Tramway runs across the page. The bridge carrying it over the main line appears in picture 46 in *Princes Risborough to Banbury*.

43.   There was no provision for passengers, not even a seat. However, one lamp is evident; the name is in the glass. The shed was occupied by a lone gatekeeper for many years. (C.L.Turner/HLHC)

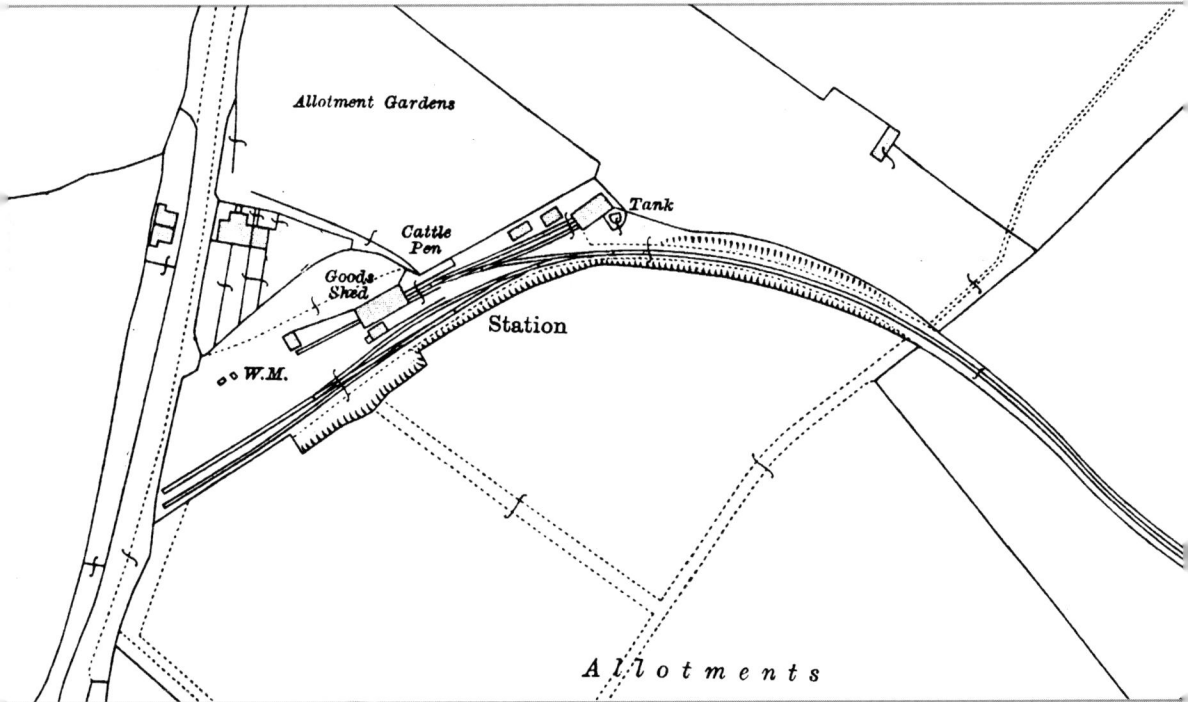

XII.   The station could be justifiably called compact, as exemplified by the 1920 survey. W.M. indicates the position of the weighing machine.

44.   Two photographs from around the end of the 19th century show Manning Wardle locos. This one has just arrived and the open door has a round head of the Met type. Brill housed 1400 souls when the line opened. Milk traffic was heavy here, as many as 30 carts bringing churns for the early morning train. (Lens of Sutton coll.)

45.　　Posed beyond the platform end, this shot seems to include almost the entire staff of the line, together with the rigid eight-wheeled coach. The goods shed on the right was the only building in the tramway days, acting as the passenger terminal and freight depot. It included the ticket office. (Lens of Sutton coll.)

46.　　No. 41 shared duties with no. 23 in the final years, working alternate weeks and resting for a week at Neasden for boiler wash-out and TLC. Devoid of condensing pipes, she was recorded on 15th March 1930. A wider cab would have meant repositioning the water fillers. The tiled roof had been above the tramway's forge. George Green (coal merchant) received about three loaded coal wagons per month in the early 1930s. (H.C.Casserley)

47.   No. 23 retained her condensing pipes, once used in the tunnels under London. Staff relax in this idyllic paradise on 8th March 1933, before taking a gentle amble through the meadows at 3.7pm. (H.C.Casserley)

48.   Weighted point levers and the cattle dock appear in this final view, which seems to include a farewell party. The notice board still proclaims Met & GC Jt. (Lens of Sutton coll.)

QUAINTON ROAD JUNCTION

49.   The line to Verney Junction is on the left of this view towards London in November 1935. On the right is the end of the GCR's London Extension and the severe kink that its expresses had to negotiate is evident. The small signal box was in use from July 1898 to about 1922, when the box seen in picture 14 took over. (Milepost 92½)

50.   The bridge seen in pictures 12 and 13 is in the background as "Director" class D11 no. 5507 *Gerard Powys Dewhurst* heads north with a Manchester express in about 1936. (D.C.Pearce coll.)

GRANBOROUGH ROAD

XIII. The 1899 survey shows the
name to include a "D".
This was not used after 1922.

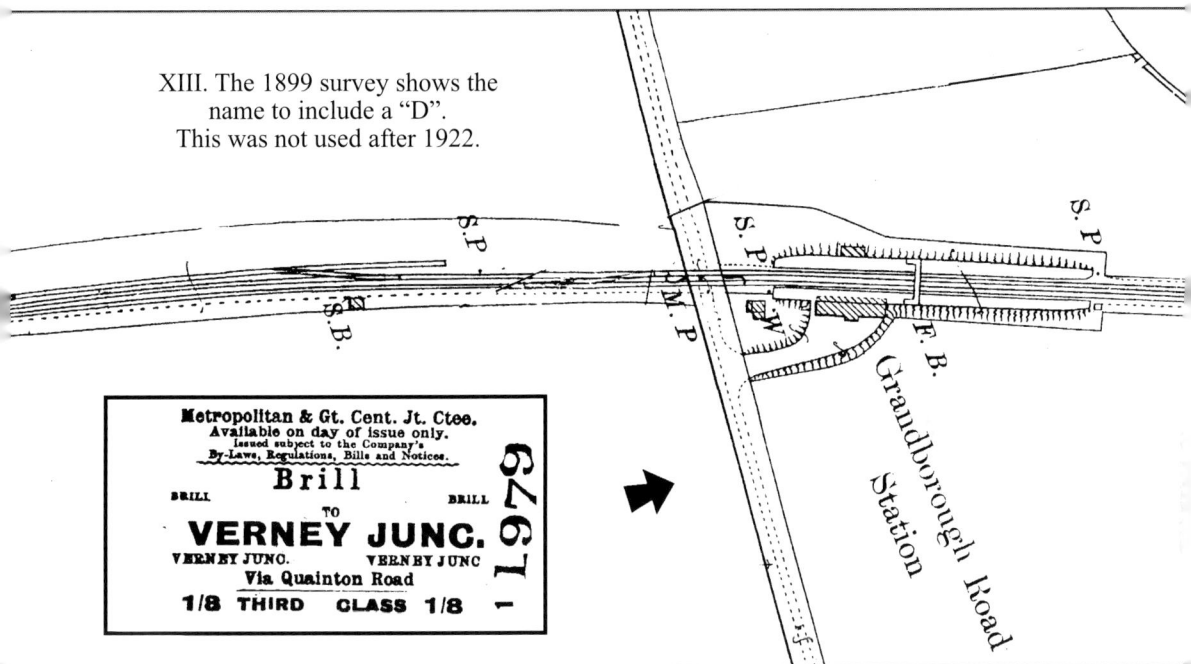

S. P.

S. P.

S. P.

M. N.

S. B.

M. P.

S. B.

F. B.

F. B.

Granborough Road Station

Metropolitan & Gt. Cent. Jt. Ctee.
Available on day of issue only.
Issued subject to the Company's
By-Laws, Regulations, Bills and Notices.
Brill
BRILL   BRILL
TO
VERNEY JUNC.
VERNEY JUNC.   VERNEY JUNC
Via Quainton Road
1/8 THIRD   CLASS 1/8

1975

51.   The buildings appear to date from the track doubling in 1891. The LNER added the cattle
dock seen in this 1933 southward view. All local traffic ceased on 6th July 1936. In the distance is
the 32-lever signal box. (R.M.Casserley coll.)

WINSLOW ROAD

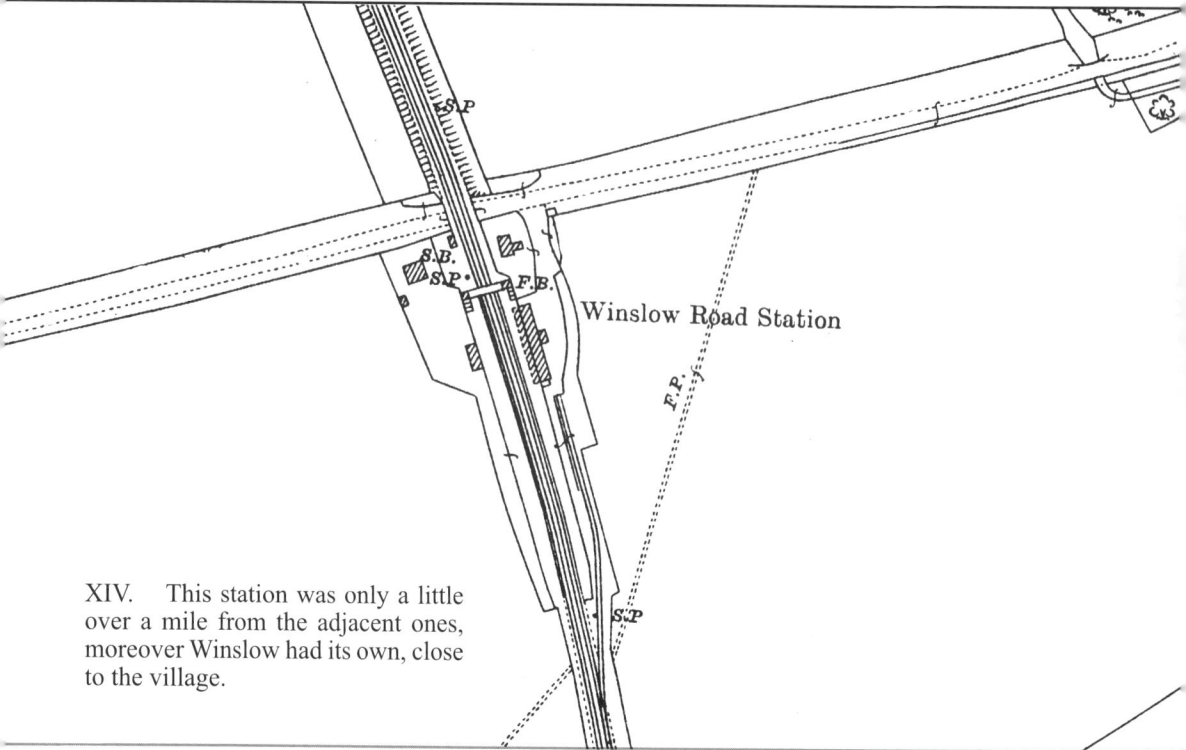

XIV.   This station was only a little over a mile from the adjacent ones, moreover Winslow had its own, close to the village.

52.   A rare view of the station in the days of single track has the solitary siding in the foreground. Light weight flat bottom rail was in use until the Met era. (G.Kerley coll./HLHC)

53. Class F7 2-4-2T no. 8307 propels coach no. 51905 towards Verney Junction on 2nd March 1936, having left Aylesbury at 6.20pm. Only 12 of these small engines were built and their large cab windows resulted in the nickname of "Crystal Palace". (H.C.Casserley)

54. As at Granborough Road, all local traffic ended when the Aylesbury service was withdrawn. Through trains ceased in 1947 and the route closed. There had been up to three Met-worked goods trains and one LNER-operated milk train daily. (Photomatic/D.C.Pearce coll.)

Verney Junction

VERNEY
JUNCTION

S.B.

S.P.

F.B.

S.P.

S.Ps

L.B

S.B.

S.Ps

Cattle P

F.P.

Station
Hotel

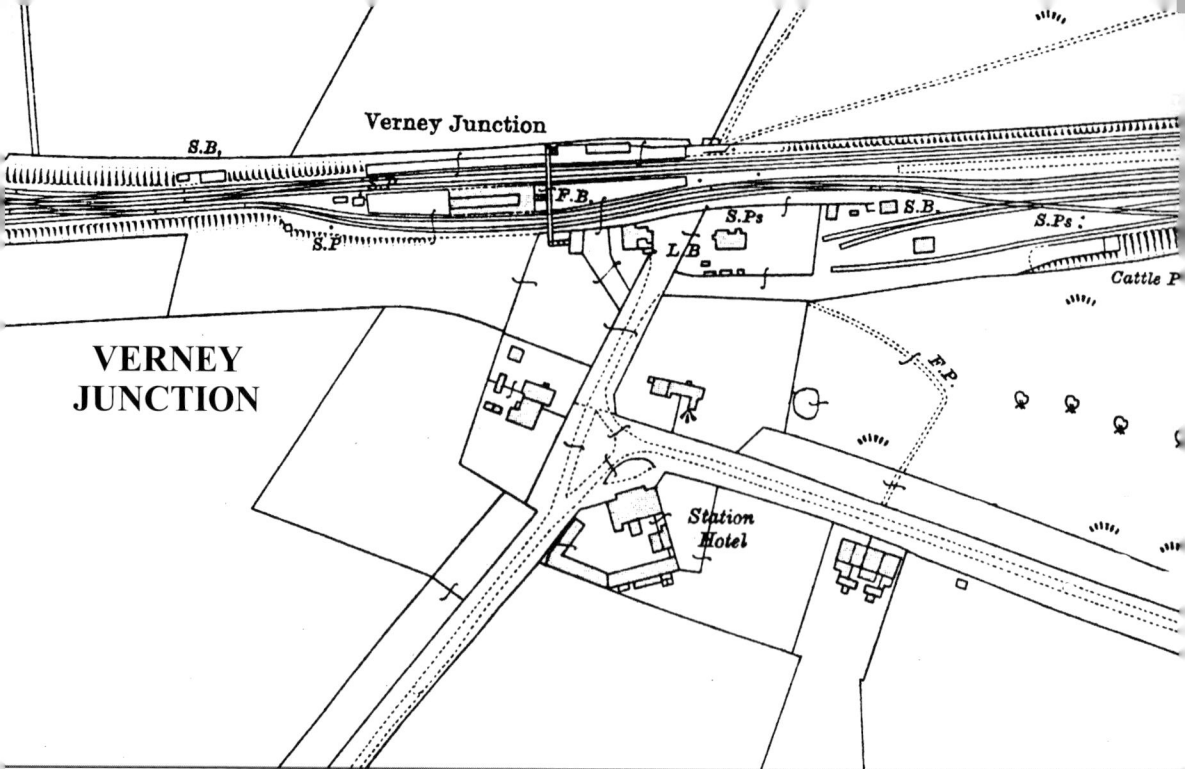

55.   No. 103 was an H class 4-4-4T of LT and is seen in 1935 about to return to London with
Met stock, known as "Dreadnaughts". In the foreground are tracks used by Oxford-Bletchley
trains until 1968. One was retained for non-passenger use and then abandoned in place in 1993,
pending further use. (P.Q.Treloar coll.)

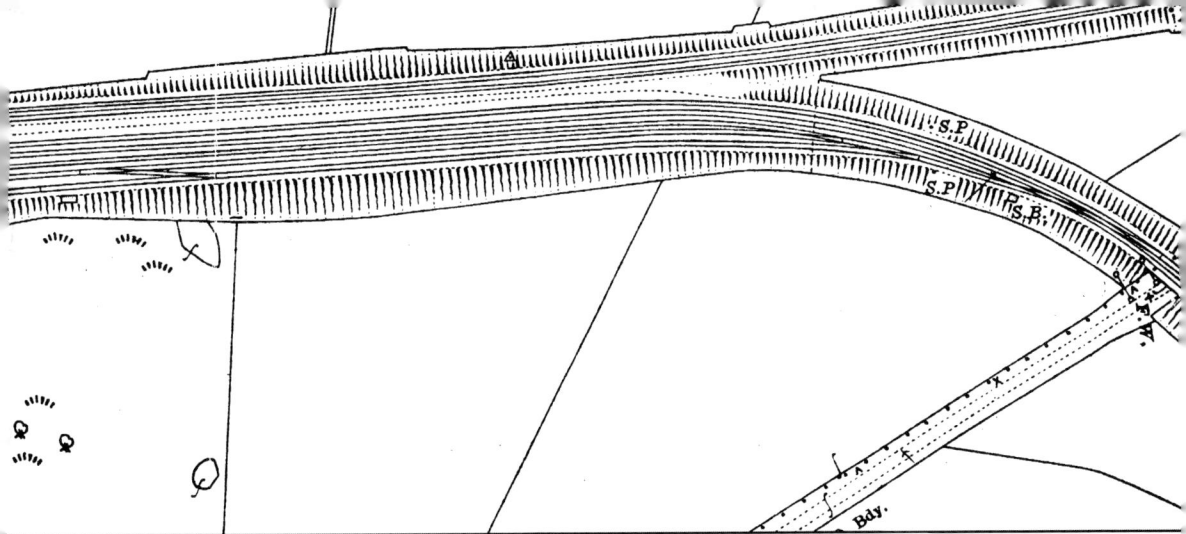

XV.   The 1923 map has the line from Quainton Road right lower and the Buckingham-Banbury route left upper. Running from left to right is the Oxford to Bletchley line of the LNWR or London Midland & Scottish Railway from that year until 1948, when it became part of the London Midland Region of BR. The station was named after Sir Harry Verney, chairman of the Buckinghamshire Railway, which built the lines north, east and west hereof. The route to Quainton Road Junction was singled on 28th January 1940.

56.   A 1953 eastward panorama from the bridge seen in the previous picture has the former Met exchange sidings, signal box and two signals on the right. Some of the lines were retained for wagon storage until 1957. LT had resumed a service between 3rd May 1943 and 29th May 1948 for war workers, but there were only one or two trips each day and they were not widely advertised. (N.W.Sprinks)

Other views of this junction can be seen in pictures 69 to 76 in our *Oxford to Bletchley* album.

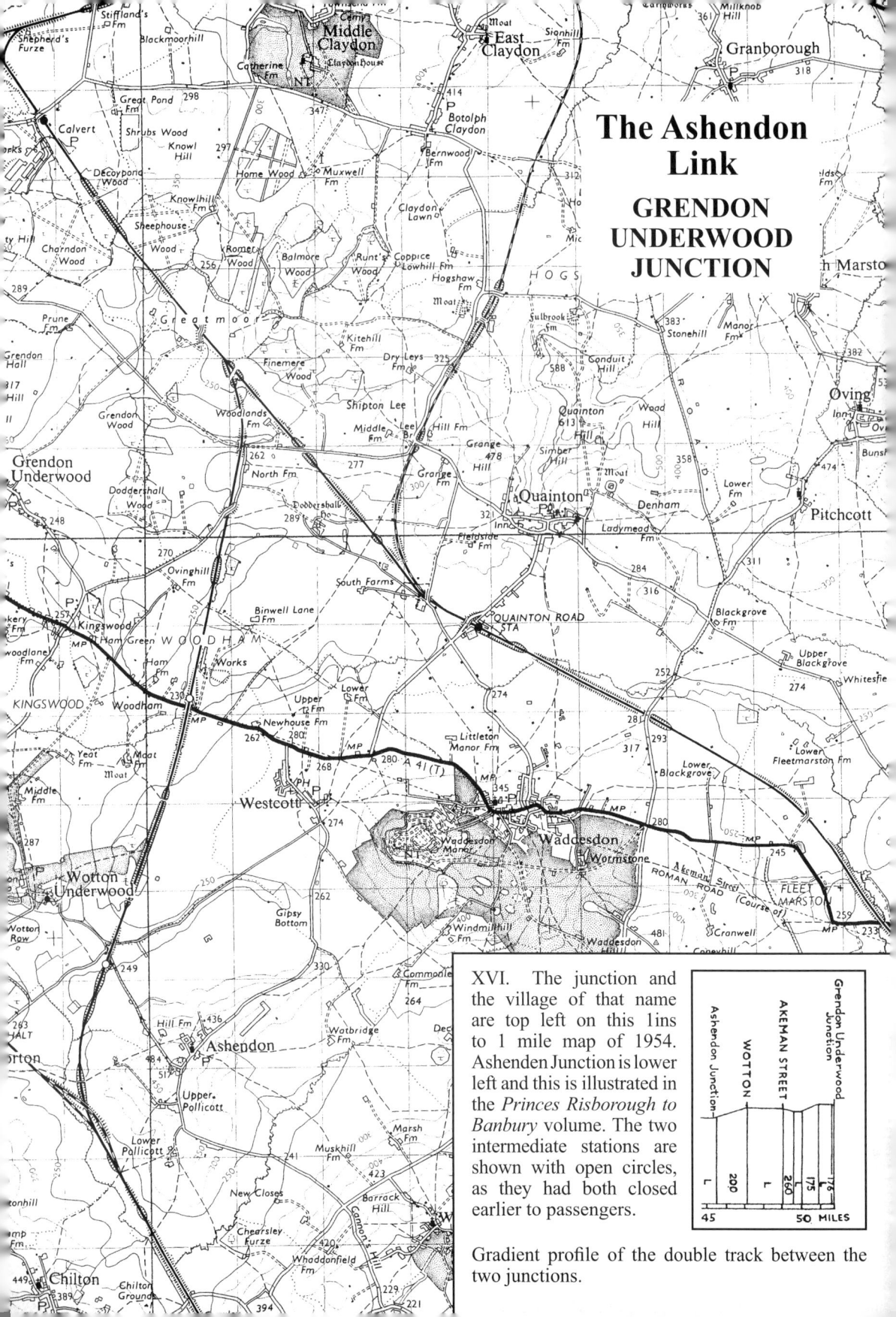

The Ashendon Link

GRENDON UNDERWOOD JUNCTION

XVI. The junction and the village of that name are top left on this 1ins to 1 mile map of 1954. Ashenden Junction is lower left and this is illustrated in the *Princes Risborough to Banbury* volume. The two intermediate stations are shown with open circles, as they had both closed earlier to passengers.

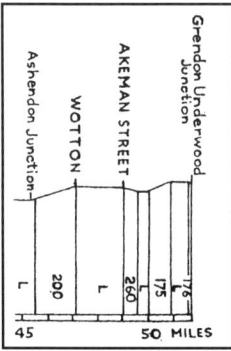

Gradient profile of the double track between the two junctions.

57a.   This southward view shows the level junction soon after it was completed in 1905. Conversely, Ashendon Junction had a flyover. The bridge in the background was for the benefit of a farmer. (Lens of Sutton coll.)

57b.   Looking north, we see yet another farm accommodation overbridge. This 1955 record reveals how smooth running was achieved on the crossing. The box had a 25-lever frame and closed on 9th December 1967. (A.Vaughan/P.M.Cowan coll.)

AKEMAN STREET

58.   A northward panorama from 1932 emphasises the generous spacing between fast and slow lines, also the great platform widths. (R.M.Casserley coll.)

XVIa.   The 1920 edition.

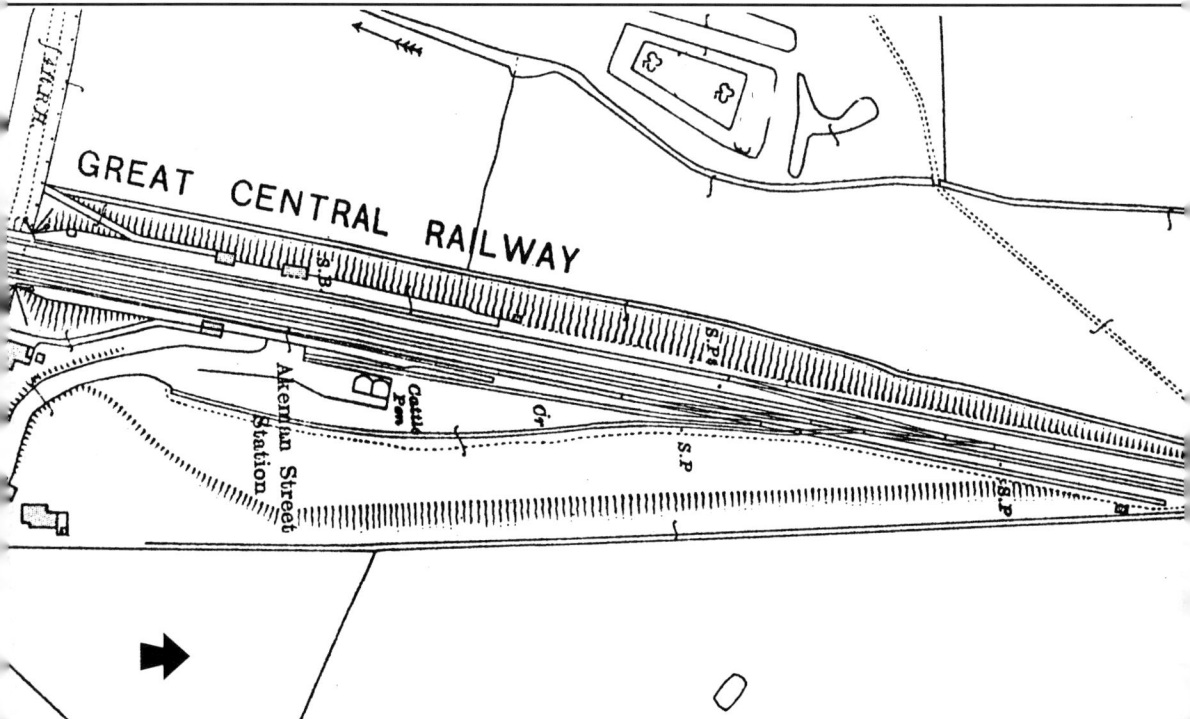

59.	The main building was on the north side of the A41 and access to the platform was via the inclined path. Passenger trains ceased to call on 7th July 1930 and there was no trace of the platforms by 1957. Goods facilities were withdrawn on 6th January 1964. (R.M.Casserley coll.)

60.	A single line from Grendon Underwood Junction was retained to Akeman Street to serve UKF Fertilisers into the 1990s. No. 31234 was recorded on 16th May 1992, with loaded vans, which have come via Bletchley. As there was no loop, the train would be propelled back to the junction and then run forward to Aylesbury, where the loco would run round. (B.Morrison)

WOTTON (LNER)

61.   Seen from the down platform, the features were common to the neighbouring station to the north. The route was clearly laid out for high speed. (Lens of Sutton coll.)

XVIb.   The 1920 edition. The Brill Tramway passes under the main line on the right.

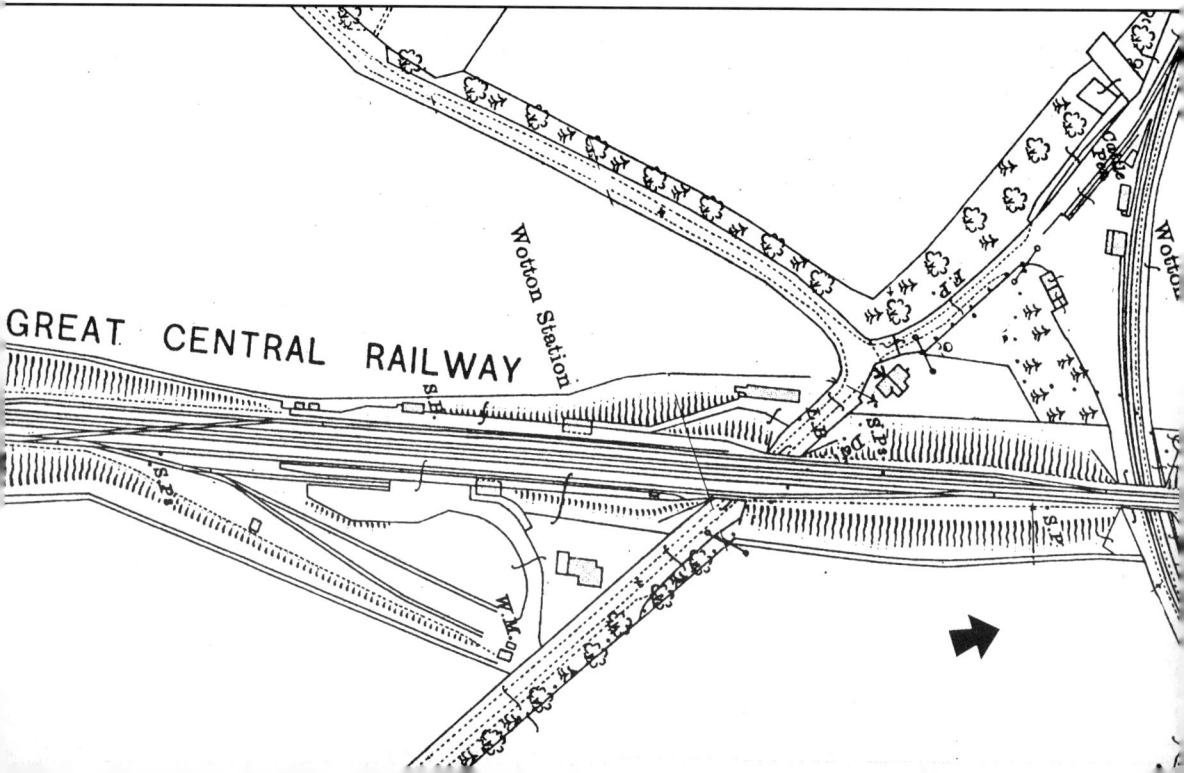

62. The loop lines were rusty when photographed on 15th April 1956. Passenger and goods facilities had been withdrawn on 7th December 1953. Until that time, there was a train from Marylebone terminating here at 7.56am and returning at 8.25. The other down train was at 7.51pm; it was 70 minutes earlier on Saturdays. However, there were *three* calling on Sundays. (R.M.Casserley)

63. The main building was still remarkably intact in July 1971. It was later converted to a dwelling, the nearby bridge having been removed in 1970. (H.C.Casserley)

Old Clay Pit

CALVERT

XVII. Although the railway constructors found Oxford Clay to be a nuisance, the GCR derived great benefit commercially from the brick traffic that followed. The 1938 map shows part of the site, which was at 300ft. above sea level. The brickworks opened in 1900 and the siding closed in December 1977, the works lasting until 1999.

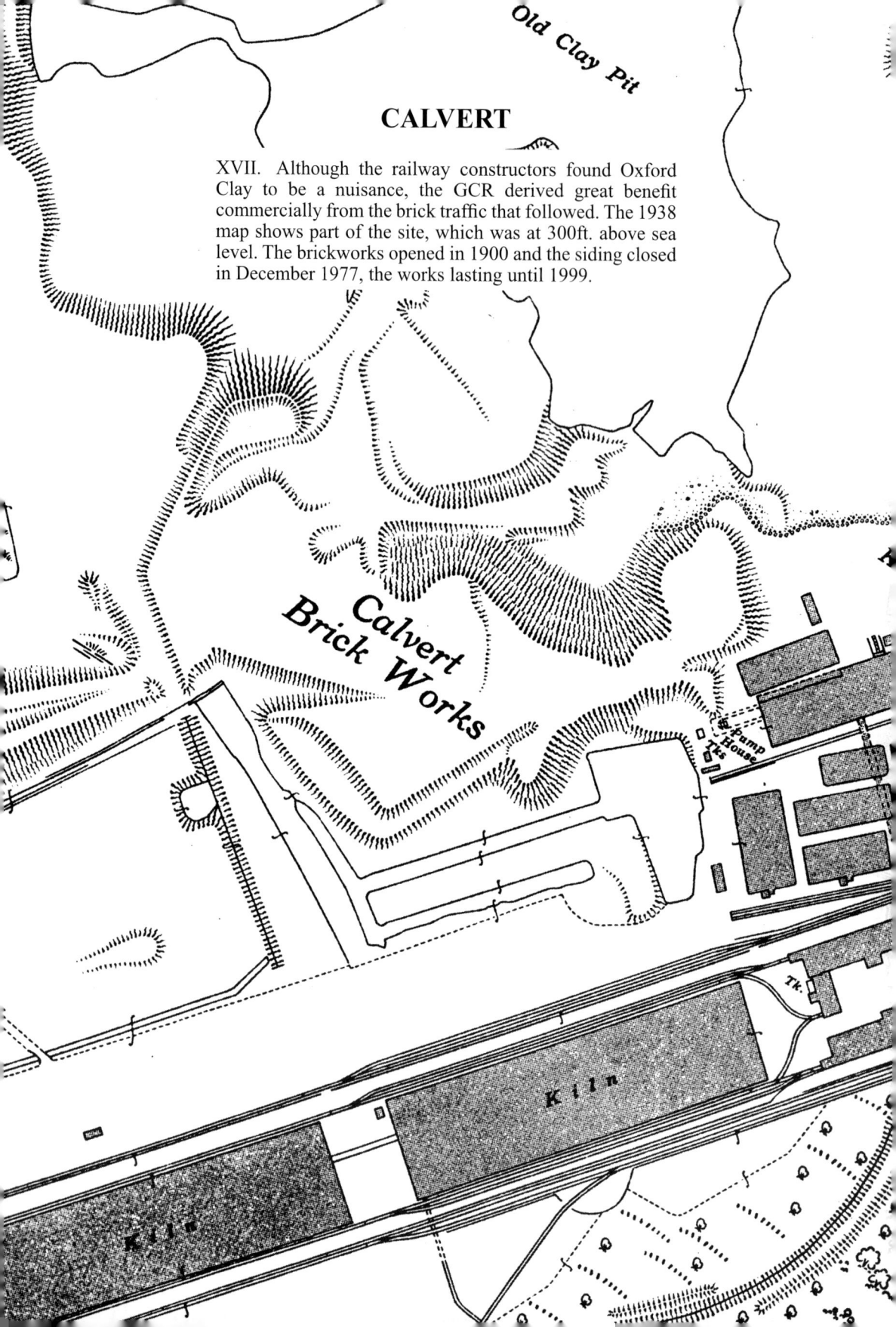

Calvert Brick Works

Pump House

Tks

Tk.

Kiln

Kiln

Kiln

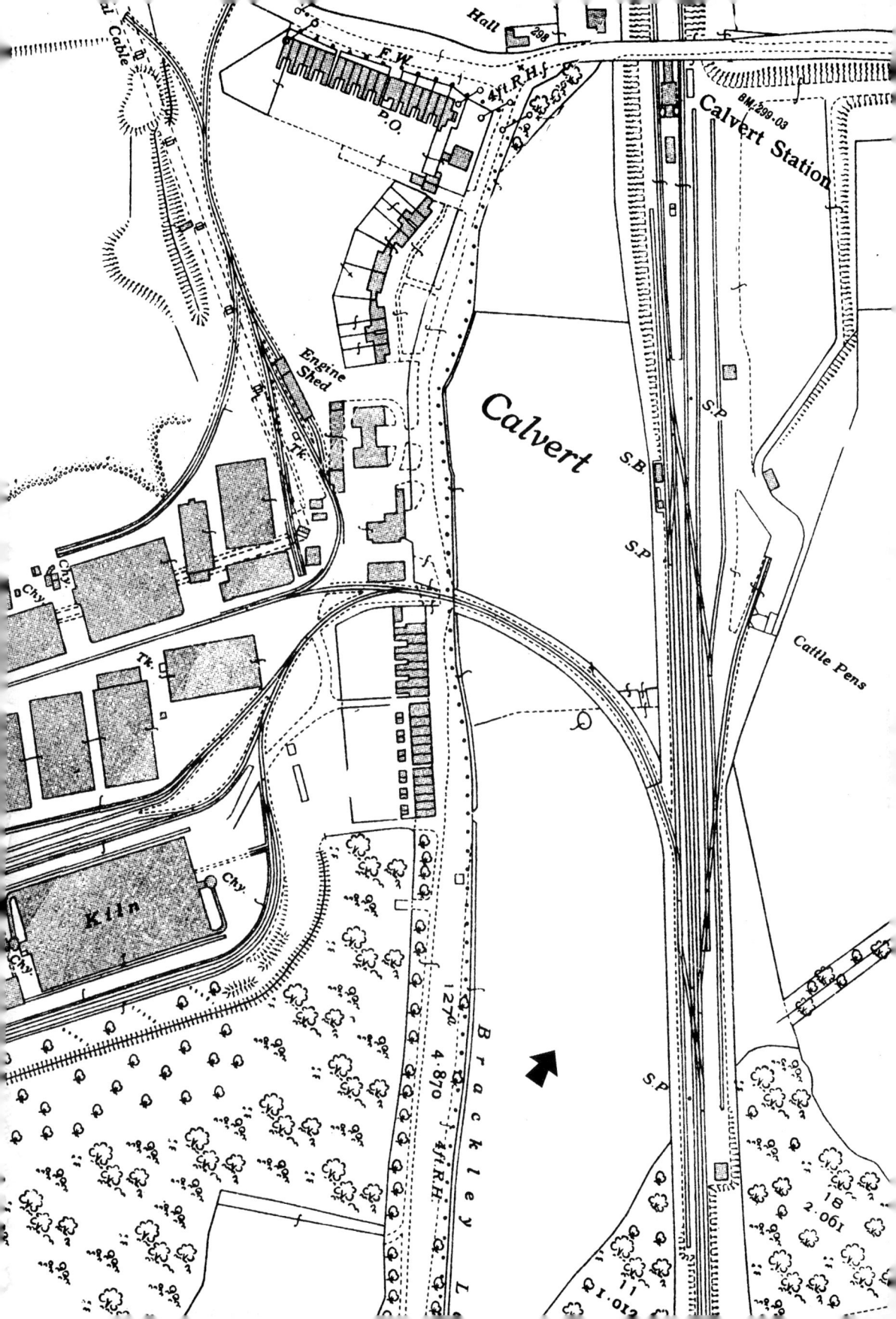

Hall

298

Calvert Station

BM 299·03

4ft.R.H.f.

F.W.

P.O.

Engine
Shed

Calvert

S.B.

S.P.

S.P.

Cable

Chy.

Chy.

Tk.

Tk.

Kiln

Chy.

Chy.

Cattle Pens

S.P.

Brackley

127·0

4·870

4ft.R.H.

1B
2.061

11
1.012

64.   The GCR specified island platforms at most stations on its London Extension, this being the most southerly. One of their disadvantages is illustrated here. (Lens of Sutton coll.)

65.   Accelerating from its stop on 22nd April 1953 is class A3 4-6-2 no. 60111 *Enterprise*, with the 1.12pm stopping train from Nottingham to Marylebone. The signal posts were more tapered than those on most other railways. (N.W.Sprinks)

66.   The gentle slope of the cuttings was due to the clay subsoil in this vicinity. The panorama is from June 1957. (R.M.Casserley)

67.   We now have two pictures from the last day on which the station was open, 2nd March 1963. This gives a good impression of the small dimensions of the booking office. (B.S.Jennings)

68.   The light was fading at 4.55pm as the last photographable up train called. It is the 4.50 from Brackley to Aylesbury. (B.S.Jennings)

69.   Most of the London Extension stations had practical, although inelegant, entrances of this type. It was recorded on 3rd June 1967, as was the next view. (J.C.Gillham)

70.   The entire goods yard is seen here; it was closed on 4th May 1964 and was subsequently used for storage of condemned wagons. In the distance is the signal box, which had 40 levers and closed on 10th December 1967. (J.C.Gillham)

71.   Southbound in May 1975 is a pair of class 25 diesel locos with a coal train from Bletchley Yard to Aylesbury Coal Concentration Depot. (Colourail)

72.   Shanks Waste Solutions operates a waste terminal at Calvert, infilling the former clay pits; traffic commenced in the early 1980s. EWS has conveyed rubbish from London (Hillingdon) via Aylesbury from the outset. Freightliner has moved material from Bristol via Oxford since April 2001 and refuse from Dagenham has been transported since May 2006. (D.C.Pearce)

XVIII. C a l v e r t station and junction are near the centre of this 1946 map at ½ inch to 1 mile. Our route runs from lower right to top left, where Finmere station is marked, but annotated Newton Purcell. The east-south spur was opened on 7th July 1940 for wartime traffic. It was double initially and singled later.

73.   This northward view has the main line rising over the LMS and the curved connection to it descending on the right. The bridge appears in picture 64 in *Oxford to Bletchley* and the northern junction of the curve is in picture 65. The Bristol "Binliner" trains were still reversing there in 2006. Calvert North Junction signal box closed on 9th September 1956 and is seen in 1955. It had 18 levers. (A. Vaughan coll.)

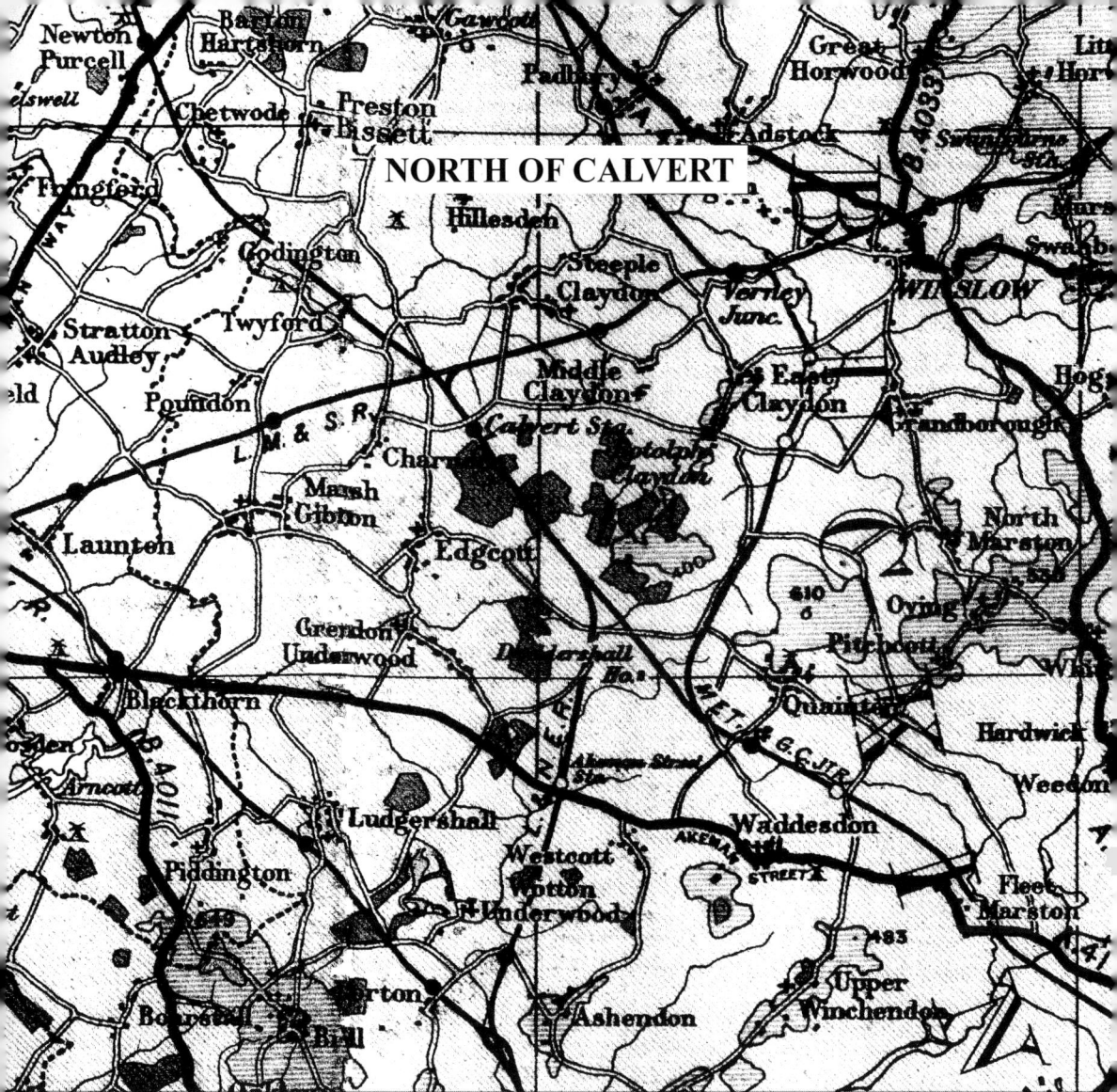

FINMERE

74.   The standard architectural plan was employed here, although the steps were up from the highway. There had been a slip coach detached here in 1923 at 7.28pm from the 6.20 Marylebone to Bradford. The coach continued, all-stations, to Woodford, where another slip had been made. The services lasted until January 1936, following an accident with it near Woodford. (D.Thompson/D.C.Pearce coll.)

XIX.   The A421 runs diagonally under the track on this 1922 edition. The small village was about one mile north along this road. The signal box (S.B.) had a 40-lever frame and lasted until 18th November 1964.

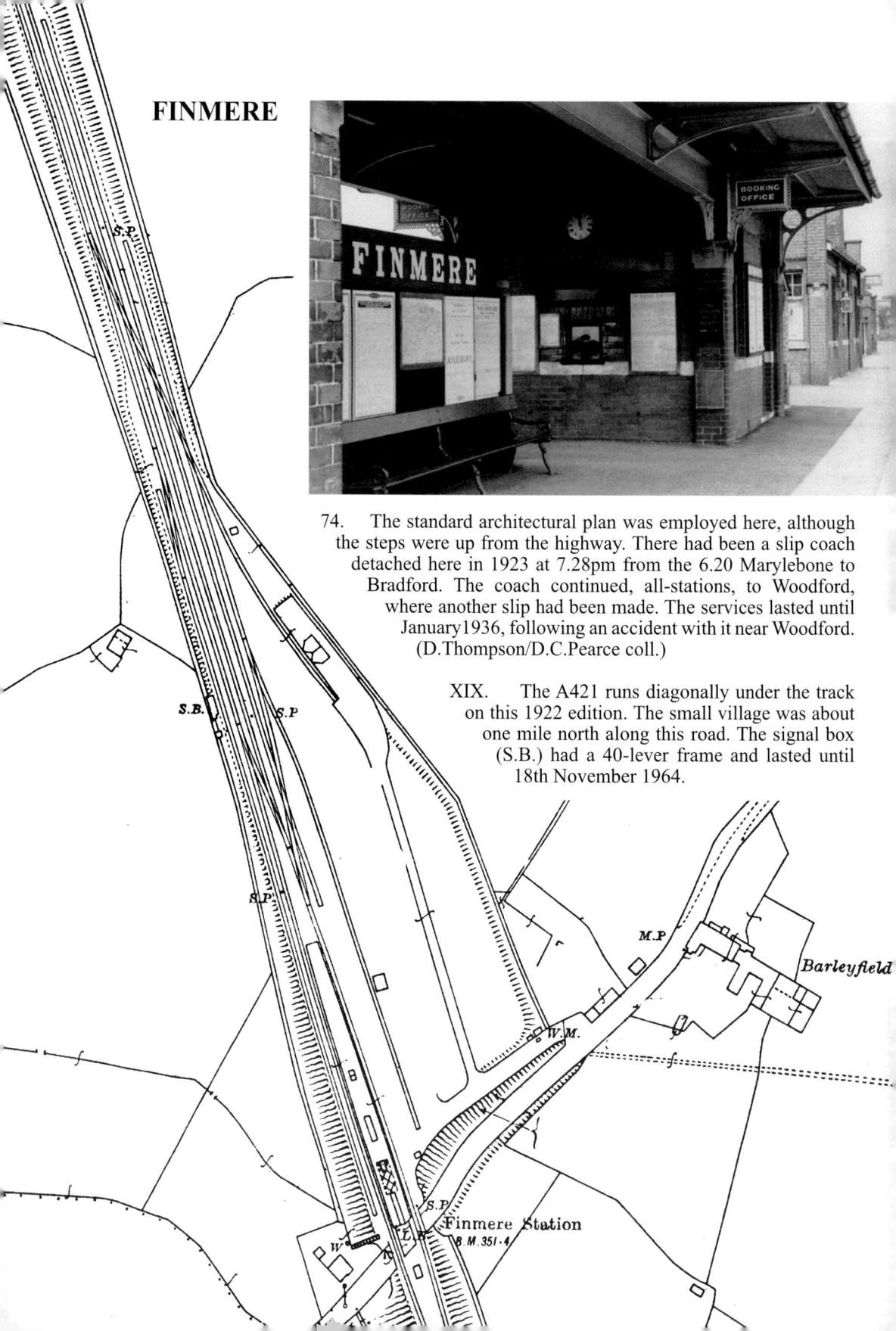

75.   Speeding through on 14th June 1962 at 9.0pm was a "Jubilee" class 4-6-0 with the 7.45pm Marylebone to Glasgow car sleeper. This was a short lived service. Stowe School generated traffic here twice every term. (B.S.Jennings)

76.   This southward panorama includes much of the goods yard, this closing on 5th October 1964. Passenger service was withdrawn on 4th March 1963. There is now no trace of the structures. (Lens of Sutton coll.)

BRACKLEY CENTRAL

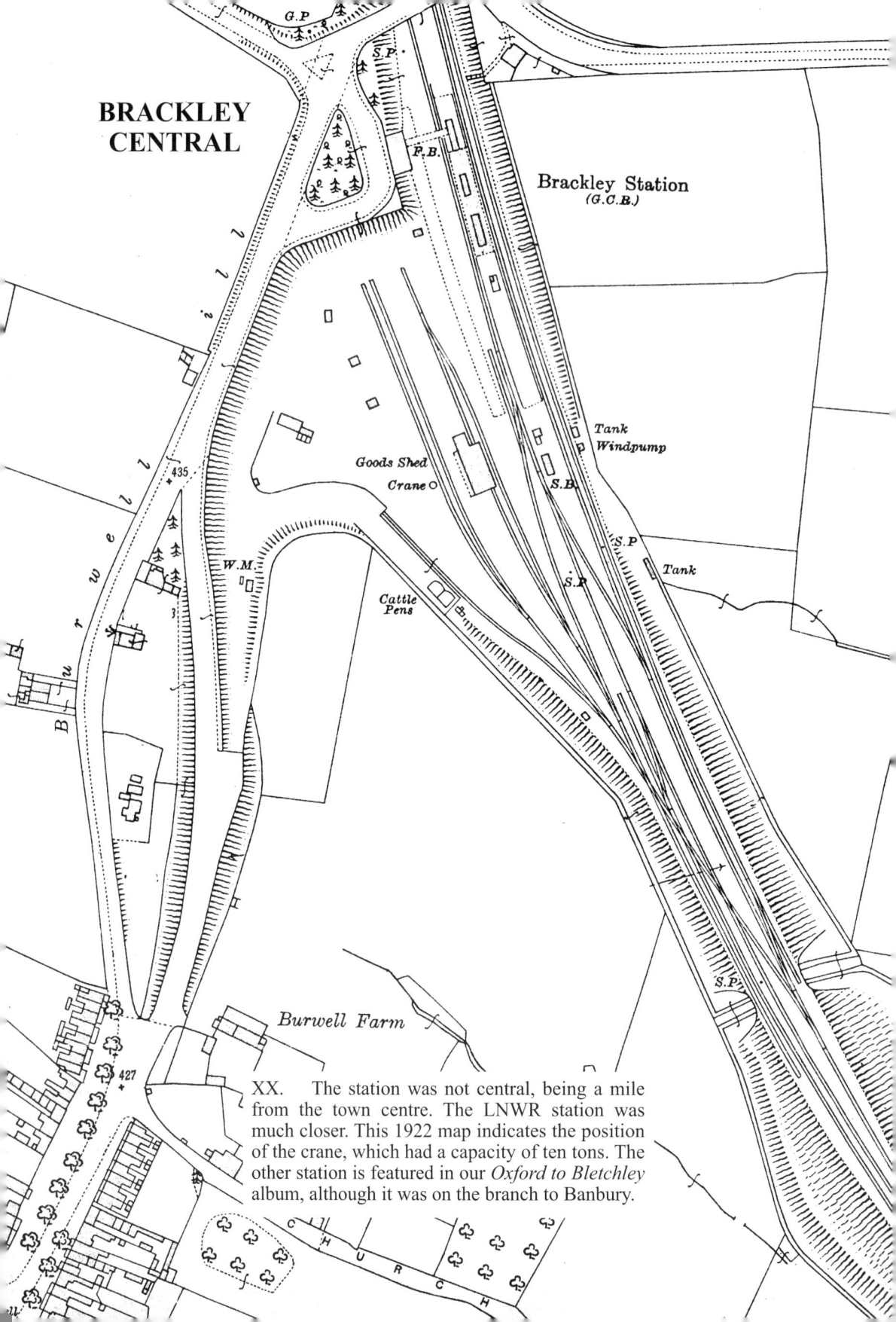

G.P

S.P.

F.B.

Brackley Station
(G.C.R.)

Tank
Windpump

Goods Shed

Crane o

S.B.

435

S.P

S.P

Tank

W.M.

S.P

*Cattle
Pens*

S.P.

Burwell Farm

427

XX.   The station was not central, being a mile
from the town centre. The LNWR station was
much closer. This 1922 map indicates the position
of the crane, which had a capacity of ten tons. The
other station is featured in our *Oxford to Bletchley*
album, although it was on the branch to Banbury.

C   H   U   R   C   H

77.   Opening day on 9th March 1899 was recorded as the first up train arrived. In the foreground is a long refuge siding, where a goods train could wait to be overtaken. (G.Goslin coll.)

78.   Being in a cutting, the entrance was at first floor level and a lift was provided as well as steps. On the left is a windpump to raise water to the tank standing beyond it.
(Lens of Sutton coll.)

79.   Waiting to depart with a down express train is class C4 4-4-2 no. 6090. The path was for staff only. The population rose from 2467 in 1901 to 3610 in 1961. (Lens of Sutton coll.)

80.   We finish our visit with three photographs from 1966, the station remaining open until 5th September of that year, unlike its neighbours. (R.M.Casserley)

81.   Features of note are the shadow-free Suggs gas lights and the generous canopies. The building continued a transport association and was used for the supply of tyres and exhausts. The platform area became the site of a factory for racing car bodies. (Lens of Sutton coll.)

82.   The goods yard had closed on 14th June 1965 and the lincs were soon lifted. In the distance is the 232yd long Brackley Viaduct, which had 22 arches. It was demolished in 1978 in favour of a bypass. This view is from May 1966; the 40-lever signal box operated in the centre of this view until 14th June 1966. (H.C.Casserley)

S.P.

HELMDON

XXI. Helmdon had a population of 516 souls in 1901 and was about half a mile to the north. The nine-arch viaduct was a little to the west of it and the LNWR station was on its northern border. This extract is from 1925.

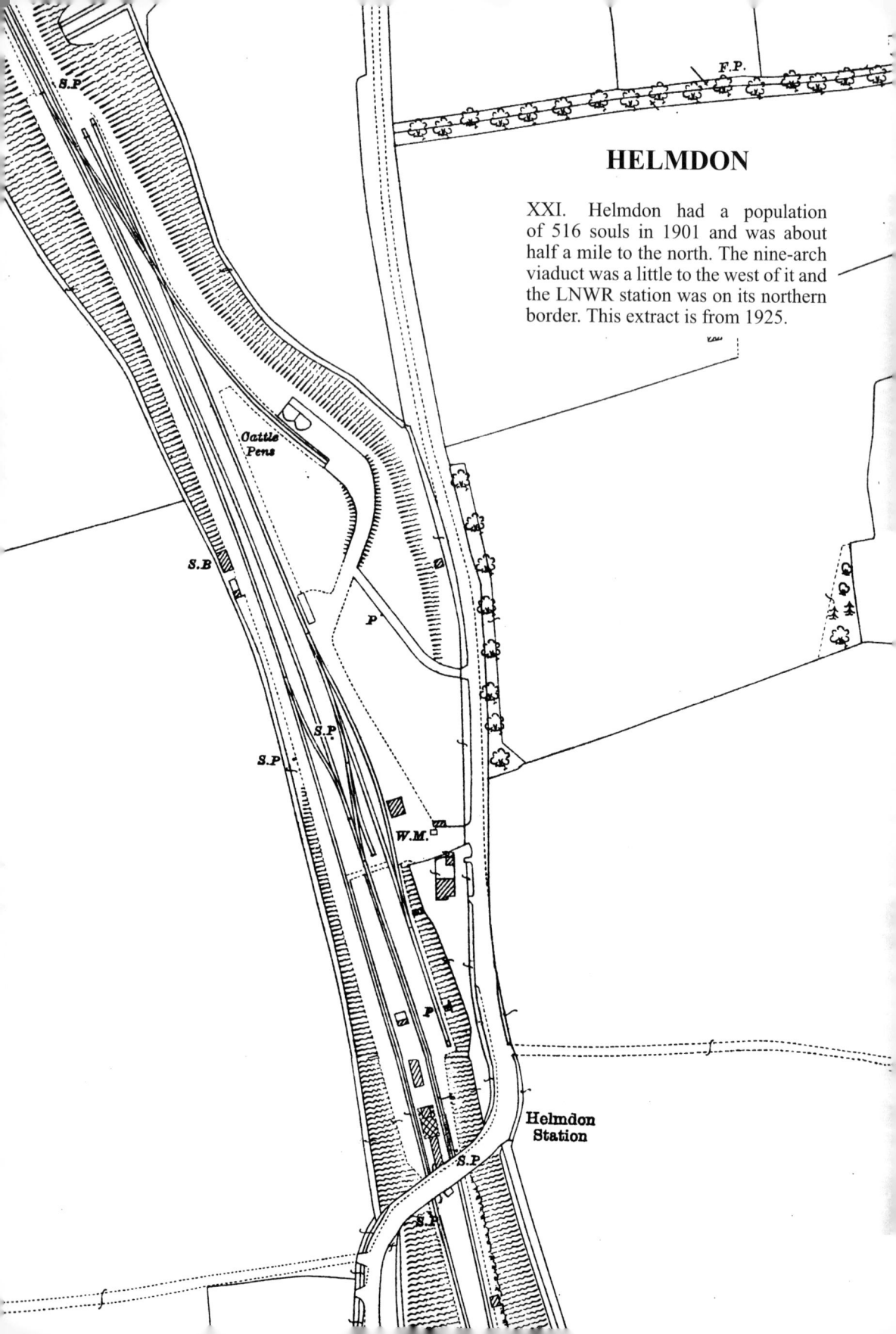

F.P.

Cattle Pens

S.B

P

S.P.

S.P.

W.M.

P

Helmdon Station

S.P.

S.P.

83.   The familiar architecture is evident in this northward panorama. The passenger service was withdrawn on 4th March 1963 and goods traffic ceased on 2nd November 1964. The former date is incorrect in two recent books on the GCR. In the distance is the 40-lever signal box, which was in use until 16th December 1964. (C.L.Mowat/D.C.Pearce coll.)

84.   The buildings were demolished in 1966, shortly before the line closed totally, but Helmdon Viaduct remained. This record is from the early 1960s and emphasises the high horticultural standards. (Lens of Sutton coll.)

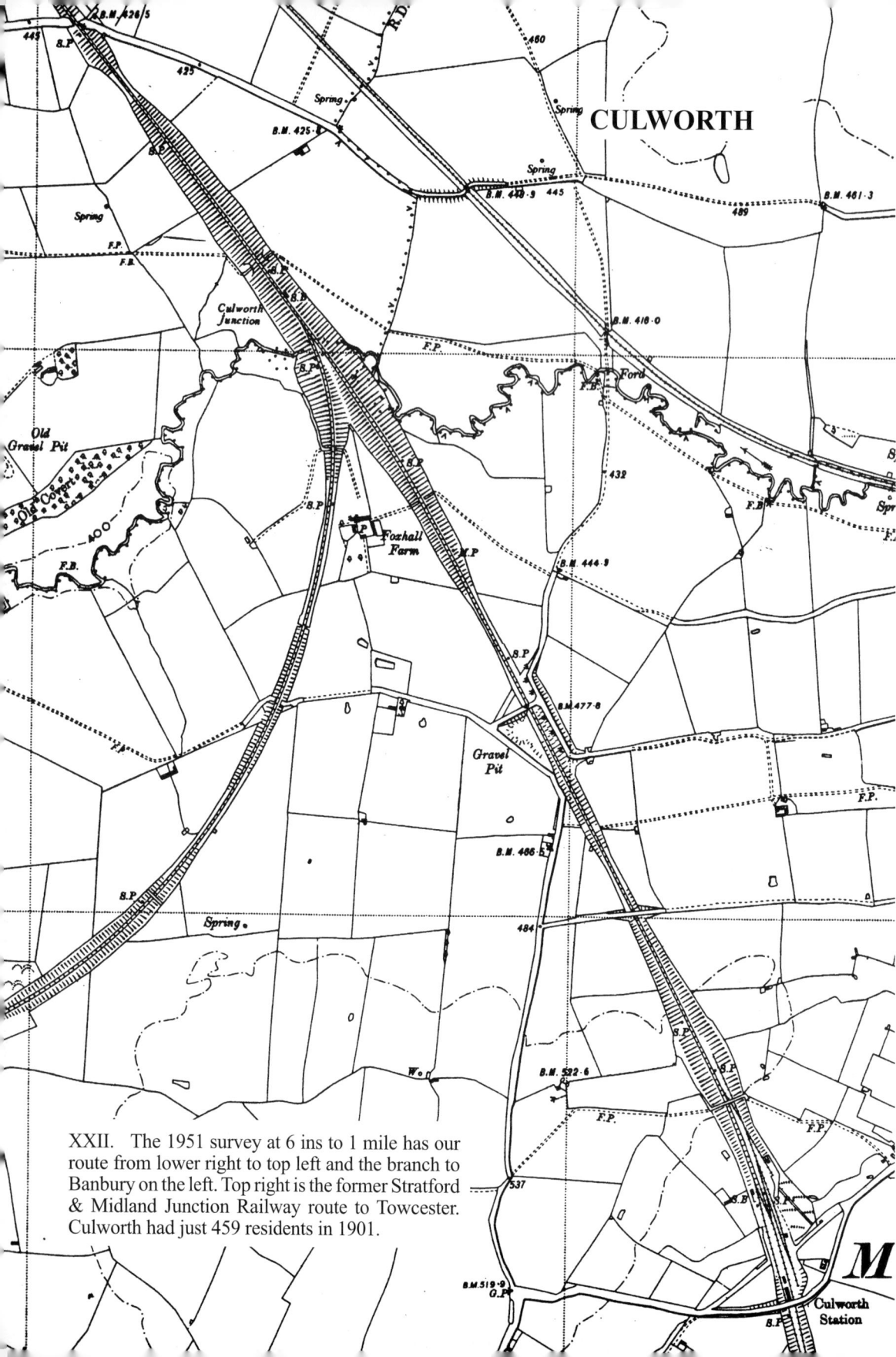

CULWORTH

XXII. The 1951 survey at 6 ins to 1 mile has our route from lower right to top left and the branch to Banbury on the left. Top right is the former Stratford & Midland Junction Railway route to Towcester. Culworth had just 459 residents in 1901.

M

Culworth Station

85. A rare shot of shunting in progress was captured through an indifferent lens in about 1930. The three-span bridge carried just a footpath. (Stations UK)

901

Met. & Gt. Cent. Jt. Ctee.
NOT TRANSFERABLE
Available for one journey only
within ... months from date of
issue.
Baker Street
(2)   TO   (S. 1
BRILL
Via Harrow
11/10 Third Class
Met. & Gt. Cent. Jt. Ctee.
Available on day of issue only.
Issued subject to the Cos' By-
laws, Regulations, Bills & Notices
Brill
(1)   TO   (S. 1
BAKER ST.
Via Harrow
Third Class 11/10
901

XXIII. The 1900 edition at 25 ins to 1 mile.

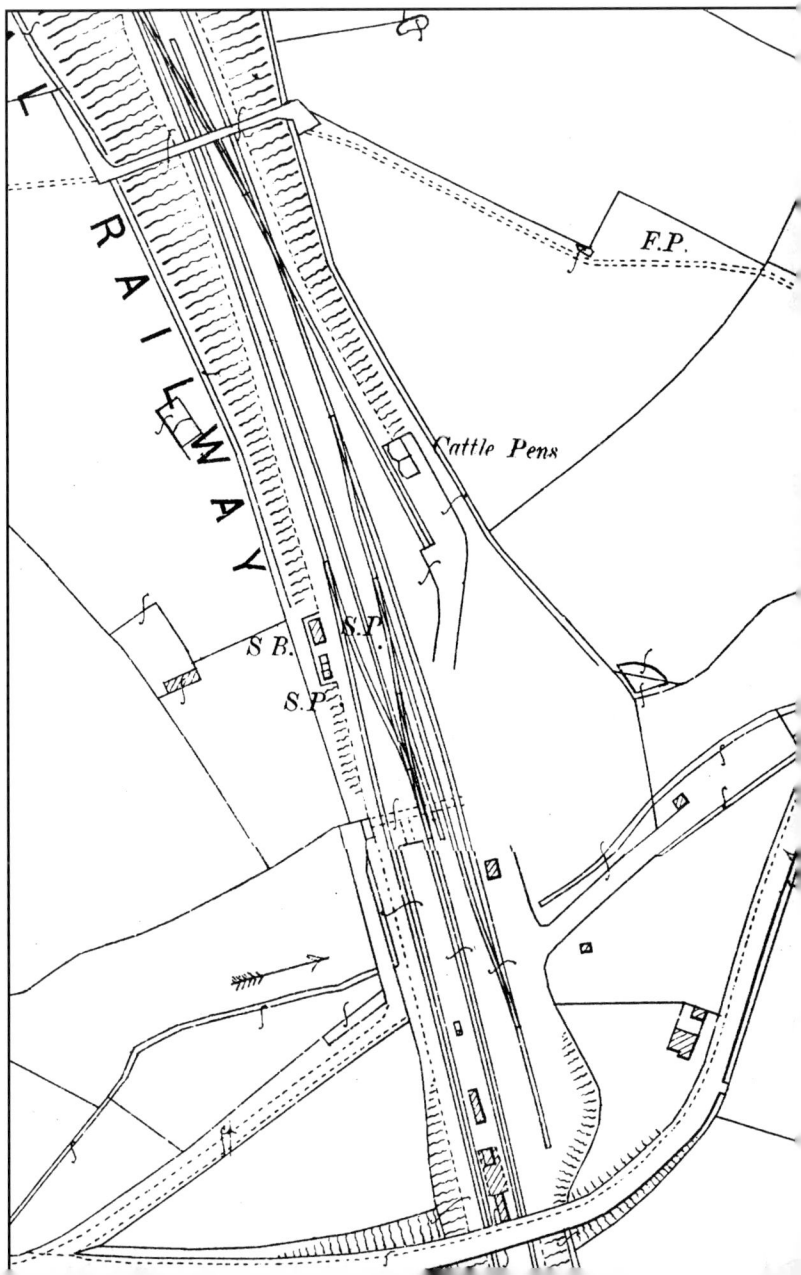

RAILWAY

F.P.

Cattle Pens

S.B.   S.P.

S.P.

86.   This 1961 picture also just includes the signal box, which had a 40-lever frame and closed on 12th August 1962. The view also contains part of the stairway down from the highway. Goods traffic continued until 4th June 1962, although it was coal only from 1958. (Stations UK)

87.   The typical entrance on the London Extension is evident on the skyline. Passenger service ceased here early, the date being 29th September 1958. The area has returned to agricultural use. (P.M.Cowan coll.)

Banbury Branch
EYDON ROAD HALT

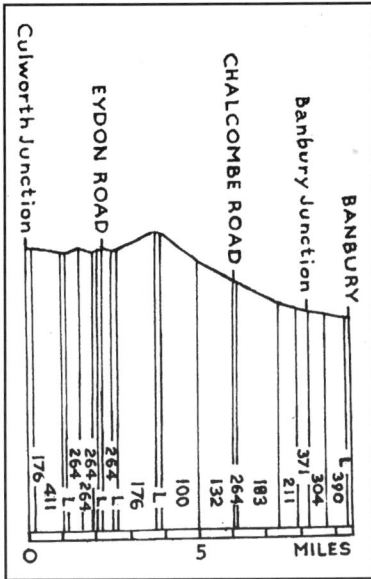

Gradient profile of the GCR line to Banbury.

XXIV. The 1900 line runs diagonally across the centre of this 1946 map, which is scaled at ½ ins to 1 mile. "Eden Road" is the pronunciation.

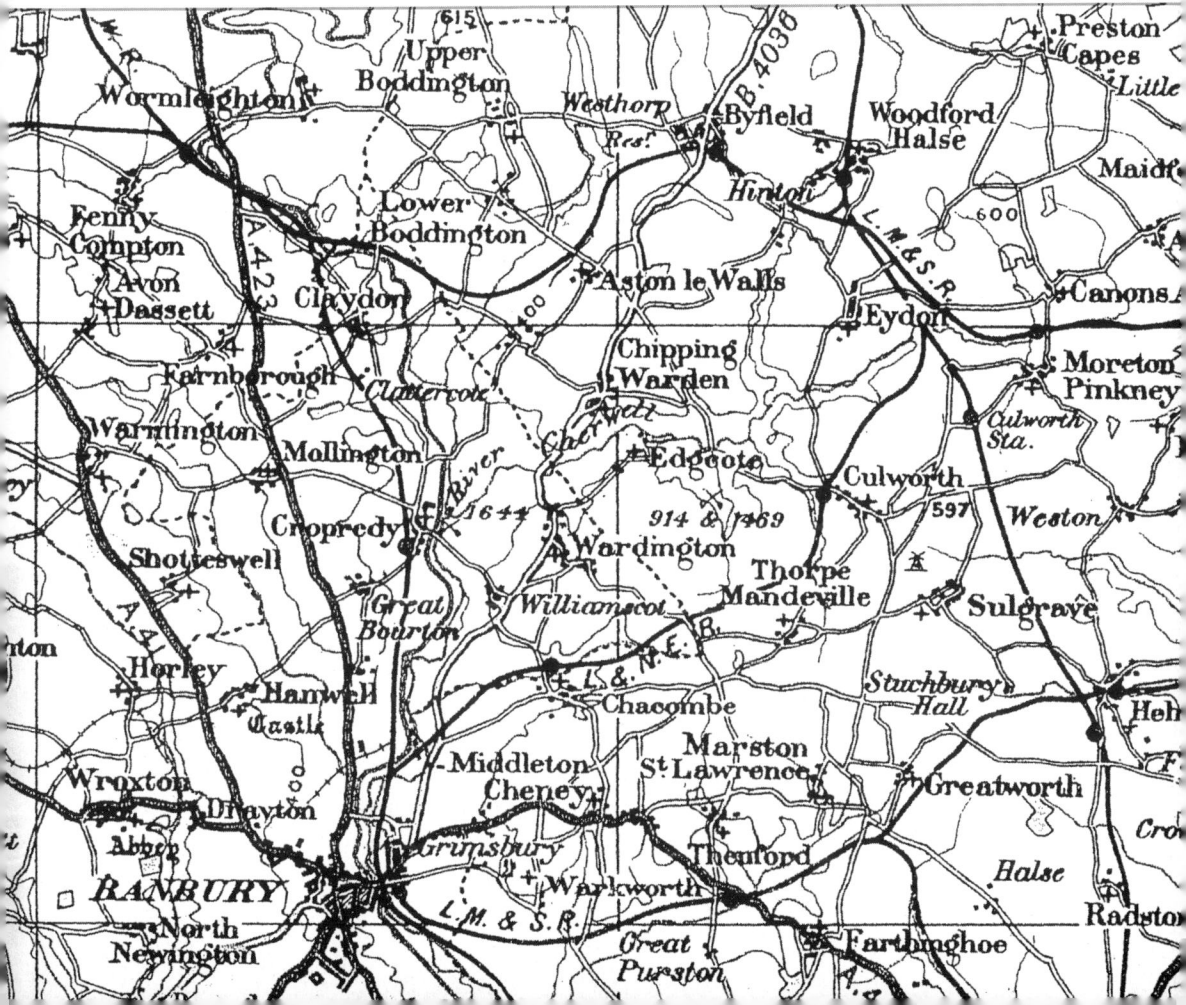

88.   The halt is to the left of the word Culworth on the map. It opened on 17th April 1911 and was initially called "Eydon Road Platform". Class J11 0-6-0 no. 64330 departs for Banbury on 31st March 1956 with the up home signal in the background. (R.K.Blencoe/D.C.Pearce coll.)

89.   The halt closed on 2nd April 1956 and a class 37 passes the remains of the signal box on 30th August 1966. Its 20-lever frame ceased to function on 21st June of that year, only the lamp room remaining intact. This is the 08.30 Newcastle to Poole express. (D.C.Pearce coll.)

CHALCOMBE ROAD HALT

90.   This halt also opened on 17th April 1911, but it closed on 6th February 1956. It was termed a "platform" initially. The route closed on 4th September 1966, but the 20-lever signal box did not function after 27th January 1965. Only nine levers were used. We are looking towards Woodford; the platform was situated just beyond the up starting signal - centre. The scouts were presumably "learning the ropes". (Stations UK)

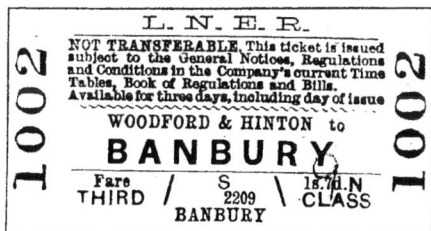

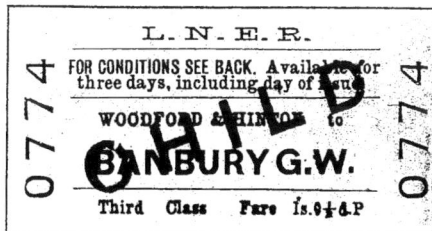

SOUTH OF
WOODFORD HALSE

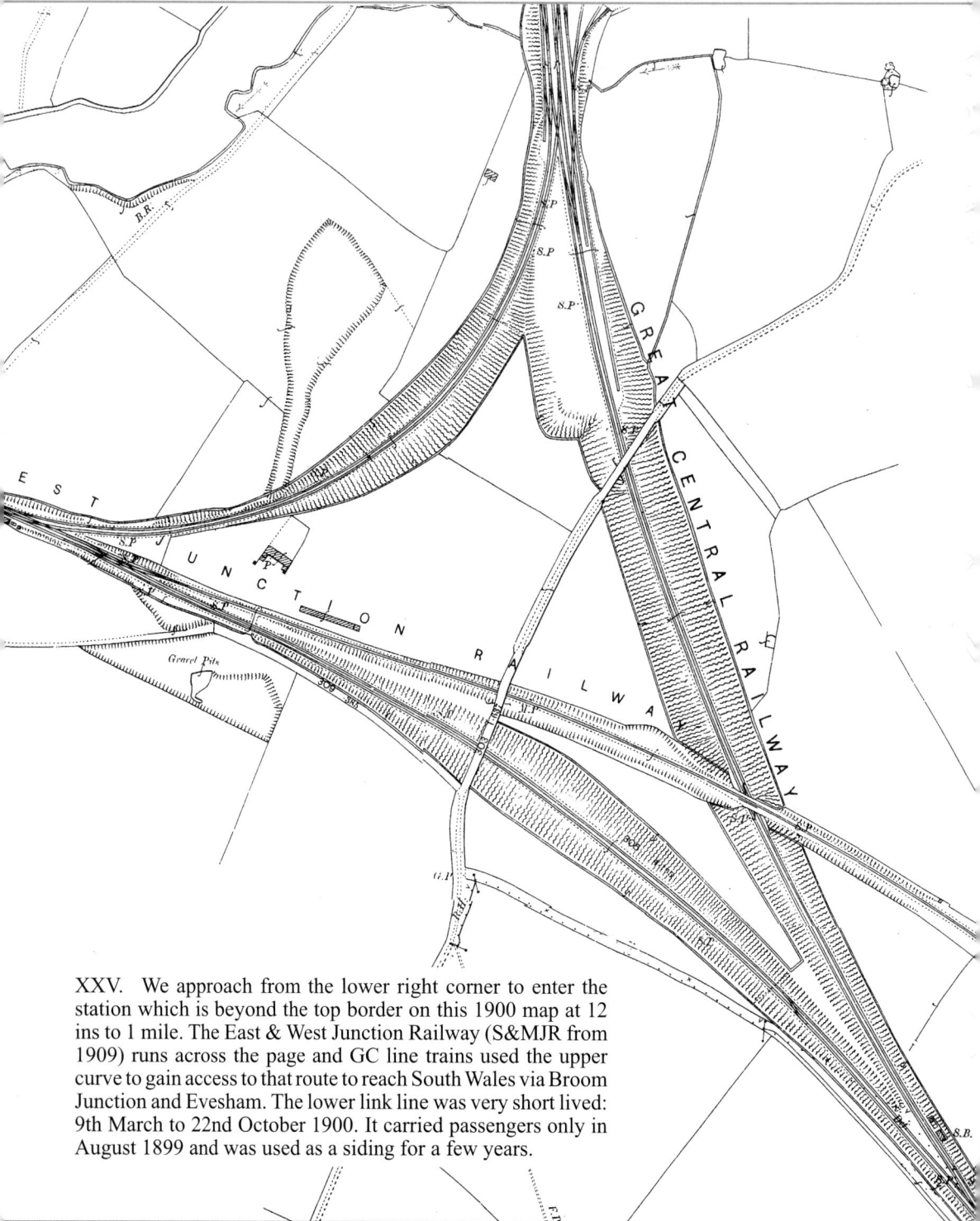

XXV. We approach from the lower right corner to enter the station which is beyond the top border on this 1900 map at 12 ins to 1 mile. The East & West Junction Railway (S&MJR from 1909) runs across the page and GC line trains used the upper curve to gain access to that route to reach South Wales via Broom Junction and Evesham. The lower link line was very short lived: 9th March to 22nd October 1900. It carried passengers only in August 1899 and was used as a siding for a few years.

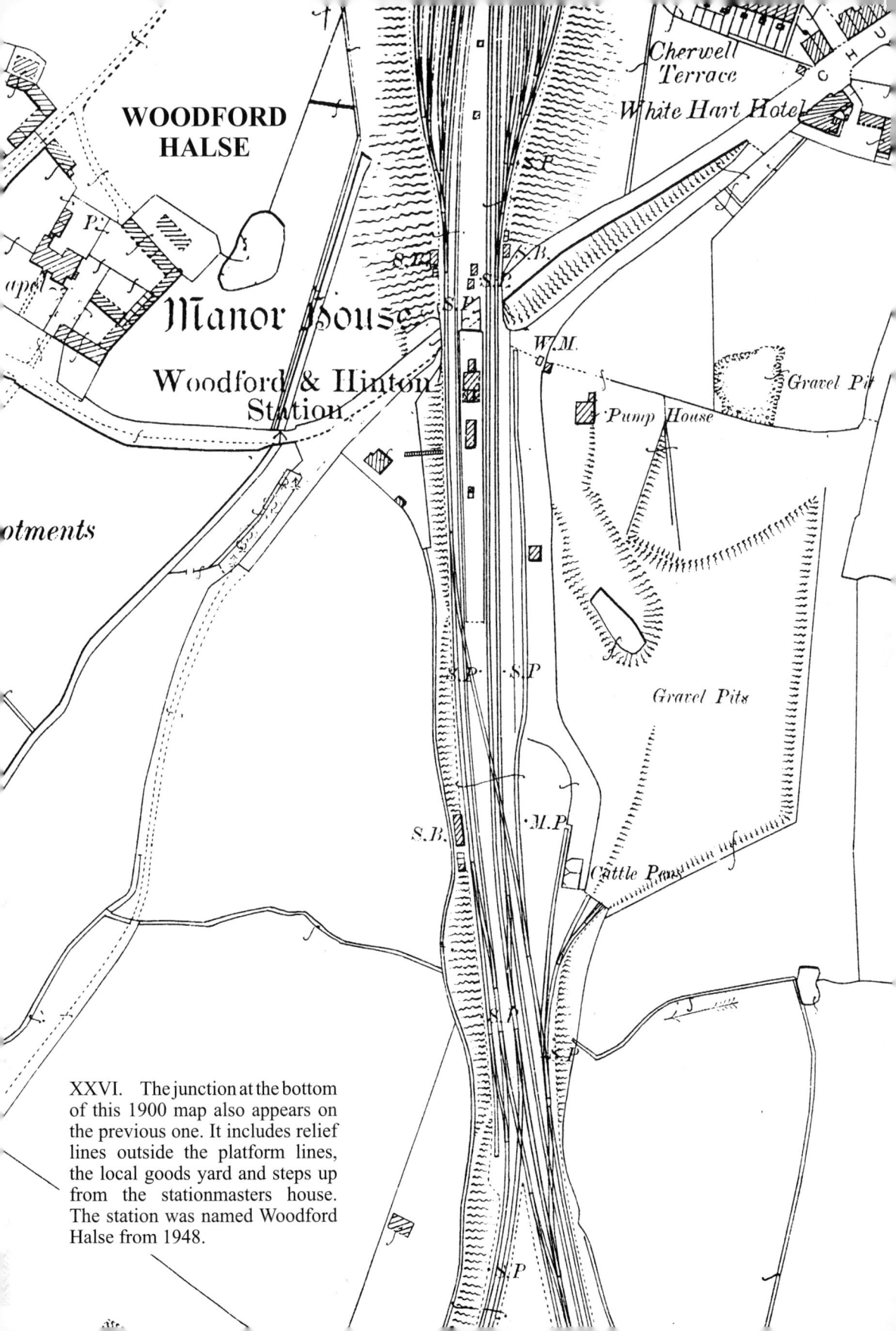

WOODFORD
HALSE

Cherwell
Terrace

White Hart Hotel

P.

Manor House

Woodford & Hinton
Station

W.M.

Gravel Pit

Pump House

otments

Gravel Pits

S.B.

M.P.

S.B.

Cattle Pens

XXVI. The junction at the bottom
of this 1900 map also appears on
the previous one. It includes relief
lines outside the platform lines,
the local goods yard and steps up
from the stationmasters house.
The station was named Woodford
Halse from 1948.

S.P.

91.	The wooden structure is an additional platform added on to the the west side of the station for local trains to Banbury and Stratford-on-Avon. On the right is the house for the stationmaster and in the foreground is a bridge over the stream, which was the source of locomotive water. (Lens of Sutton coll.)

92.	A postcard view features an up train hauled by GCR class 8B 4-4-0 no. 361. The sign offers a wide range of destinations: Banbury, Oxford, Reading, Aldershot, Southampton, Portsmouth, Bournemouth, Weymouth, Cheltenham, Bath, Bristol, Cardiff, Exeter, Plymouth, Dover, Folkestone and Stratford on Avon. (Lens of Sutton coll.)

93.   Standing at what became known to railwaymen as the "Wooden platform" on 20th July 1946 is LMS 0-6-0 no. 3520 with the 8.20am to Stratford-on-Avon. The name shown was used until 1948. All the names were removed during World War II, although leaving the others could have confused the enemy. (H.C.Casserley)

94.   A northward panorama from the island platform in the 1950s includes both "Old Yards" and No. 3 box. It had 29 levers and was taken out of use on 26th September 1965. A local passenger train to Banbury waits in the centre siding, a service which continued until 1963. (A.W.V.Mace/Milepost 92½)

95.   The up signals were still of GCR pattern in 1952. The crane was of two-ton capacity. No. 1 Box was at the north end of New Up Yard and No. 2 was between the down yards. (P.J.Garland/R.S.Carpenter coll.)

96.   Class B1 4-6-0 no. 61001 is on an up parcels train in September 1954. The pump house is on the right and the vans are near the weigh house. (A.W.V.Mace/Milepost 92½)

97.   Looking south, we have No. 4 Box in the distance and the roof over the stairs from the road on the left. The bridge wing wall is on the right; it also appears in picture 91. (P.M.Cowan coll.)

98.   The 3.5pm southbound stopping train awaits departure on Sunday 10th May 1953. This train normally ran to Marylebone, but on this date was terminating at Calvert, with a bus connection to Aylesbury, due to an engineering occupation at Grendon Underwood Junction. LMS-type 2-6-0 no. 43144 has two ex-LNER non-corridor coaches, with an ex-GC coach at the rear. The sign had been altered rather crudely. (N.W.Sprinks)

99. A southward panorama in 1959 from the end of the island platform includes No. 4 Box and the quadruple track, which continued south to the junction. This is to the right of the coaches. On the left is the cattle dock.
(B.W.Leslie/GCR Soc.)

100. The entrance was inevitably gloomy, being between two double track bridges. It was photographed near to closure in 1966.
(Lens of Sutton coll.)

101. The wooden platform had been changed to concrete slabs in 1956, but there is now no trace of the station, at rail level. Details were not recorded, but the LMR sign indicates that it is post-1958.
(D.C.Pearce coll.)

NORTH OF WOODFORD HALSE

XXVII. This map continues from the previous one, but with a gap of 200yds owing to the length of the marshalling yards. Two similar ones were added further north in 1941. The turntable shown was replaced by a triangle in 1942. The four yards closed in June 1965.

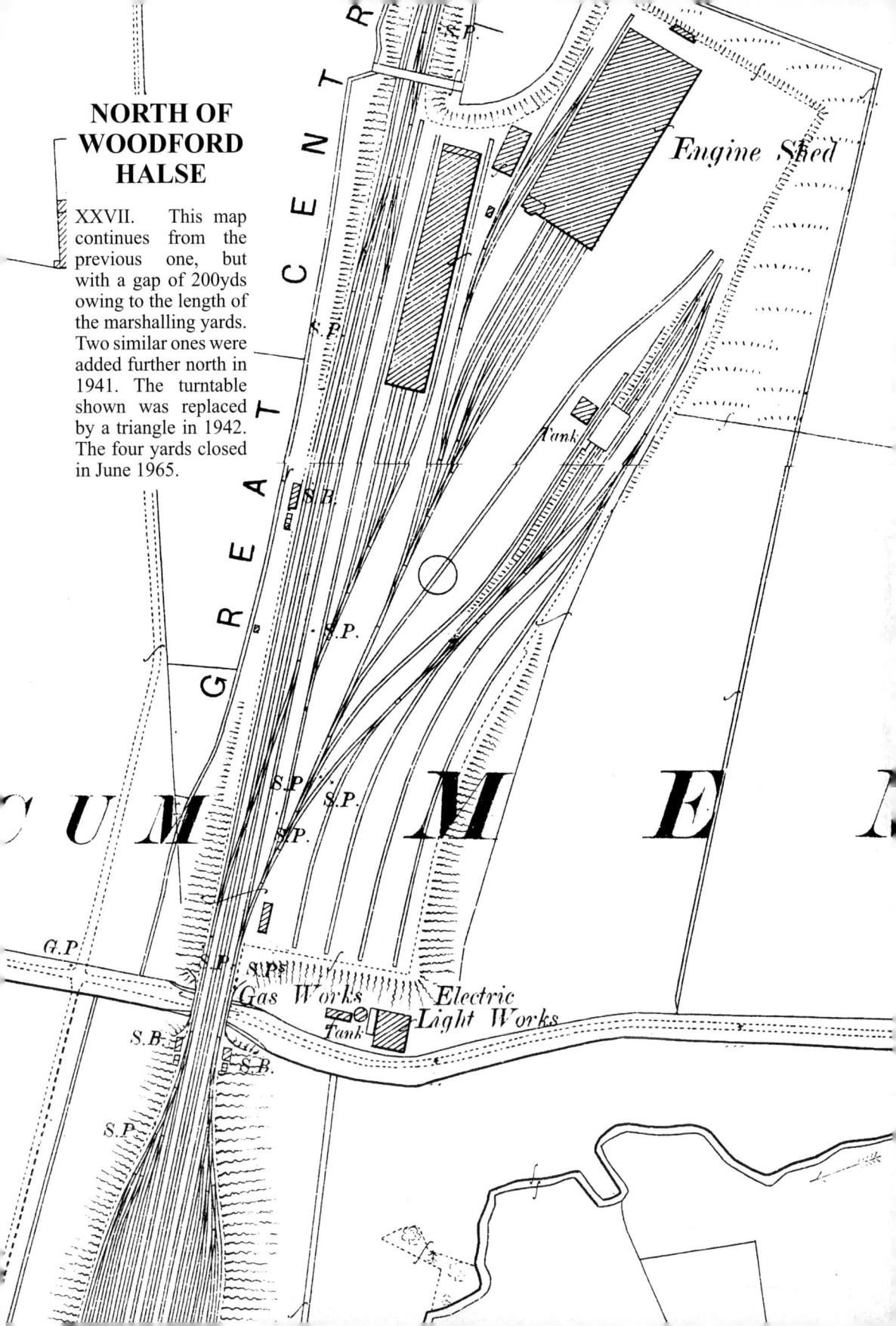

Engine Shed

Tank

G R E A T   C E N T R

S.P.

S.P.

S.P.

S.P.

S.P.

S.P.

S.P.

S.P.

S.P.

S.P.

CUM M E

G.P.

S.B.

S.B.

Gas Works

Tank

Electric Light Works

102.	In the last year of the LNER, the engine allocation was 7 B1s, 7 K3s, 17 O7s, 9 J11s, 4 J5s, 3 J50s, 2 L3s and 2 N5s. The photograph is from 17th July 1955; this was a Sunday and so more engines were to be seen than normal. At the fore is no. 90365, an ex-WD 2-8-0. (B.Harrison/ D.C.Pearce coll.)

103.	The shed code under the Eastern Region was 38E and the LMR used 2F later. Featured is class J39 0-6-0 no. 64747 on 3rd October 1964. It had been withdrawn in 1962 and was serving as a stationary boiler. Seen above it is the water tank, which surmounted the coal stage. This had been made redundant by the coaling plant in the background in 1935. The building to the left of it housed the sand driers.	(K.C.H.Fairey/ D.C.Pearce coll.)

104.	Working from here in 1959 were 2 4MTs, 3 3Fs, 3 V2s, 5 B1s, 8 K3s, 1 J10, 3 L1s and 26 WDs. By 1965, there were only 2 4MTs, 4 5MTs and 12 8Fs. The complex is seen from a down train on the last day of operation. The new roof on the massive loco shed (left) dated from 1945. Right of centre is the power house and extreme right is the rear of the carriage and wagon repair shop. Factory units now occupy much of the area. (Gulliver/ D.C.Pearce coll.)

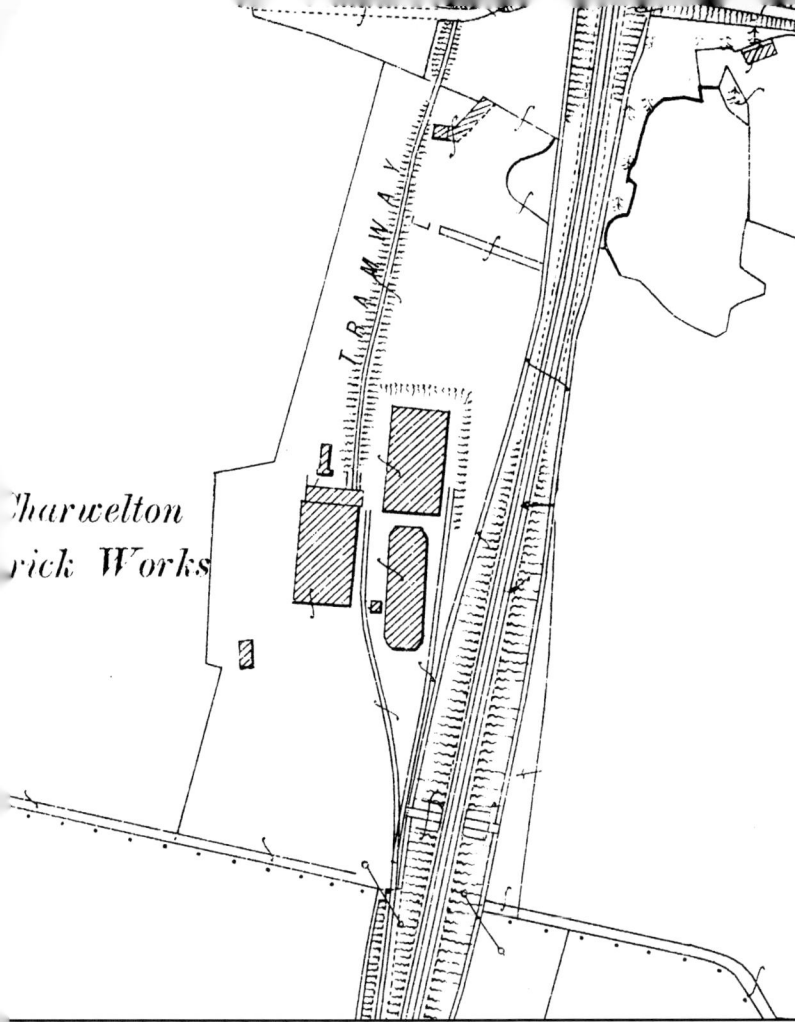

SOUTH OF CHARWELTON

Charwelton
rick Works

XXVIII. The 1900 survey shows a single siding dividing into two after passing through the firm's gate. It was listed as in use in 1938.

105. To speed up the expresses, water troughs were installed, these coming into use on 1st July 1903. London to Sheffield non-stop was then possible. We witness cx-ROD class O4/3 2-8-0 no. 6262 working an up freight train.
(G.W.Goslin coll.)

CHARWELTON

XXIX. The 1900 edition reveals that a stream passes under the station building and under the bridge north of the goods yard. The population of the village was 182 in 1901. The photos show that siding extensions took place.

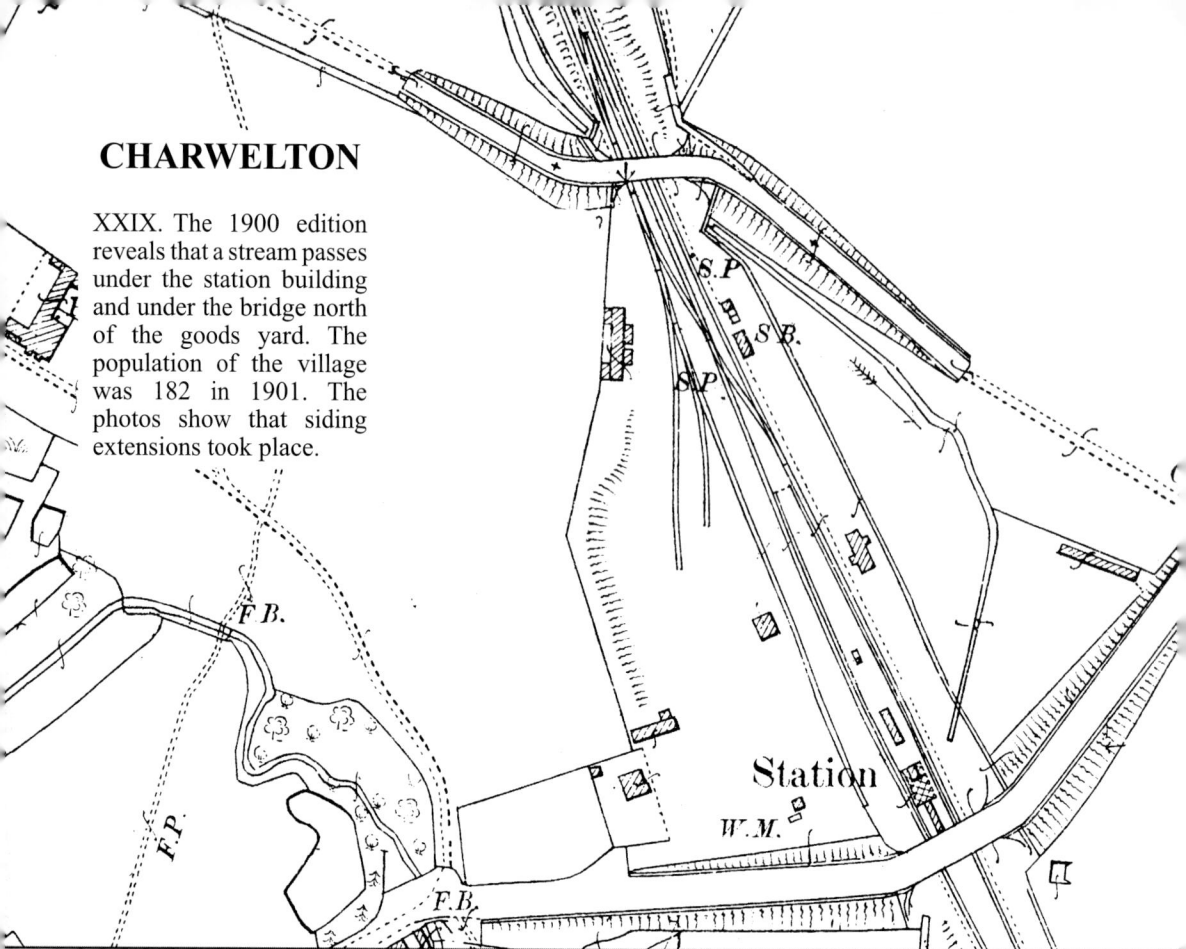

S.P.

S.B.

S.P.

F.B.

F.P.

Station

W.M.

F.B.

106. Class D11 4-4-0 no. 5505 *Ypres* heads south with a stopping train on 3rd July 1937. Most structures were built with four tracks in mind. However, the line on the left is only a refuge siding, an extension of one in the goods yard. (L.Hanson/P.Q.Treloar coll.)

107. We look north from the farm bridge at the top of map XXIX and witness class O4 2-8-0 no. 5012 blowing off after reaching the summit level on 4th July 1941. The signals in the distance are for the up loop. North of the 2997yd long Catesby Tunnel is the 12-arch Catesby Viaduct. Further north was Staverton Viaduct and Willoughby Viaduct. (H.C.Casserley)

108. A peep from the road bridge includes the weighing machine, two sack trucks, a trolley and staff transport. Both local passenger and goods services were withdrawn on 4th March 1963. (Lens of Sutton coll.)

109. Another photograph from about 1962 and this includes the line to the ironstone quarry of the Parkgate Iron & Steel Company. It was in use from May 1917 until November 1961. Its siding passes over two diamond crossings. A light engine stands at the down home signal. Staverton Road was the next signal box north; it had an up refuge siding and its 20-lever frame was not used after 14th June 1965. The box shown had 40 levers and functioned until January of that year. (Lens of Sutton coll.)

BRAUNSTON & WILLOUGHBY

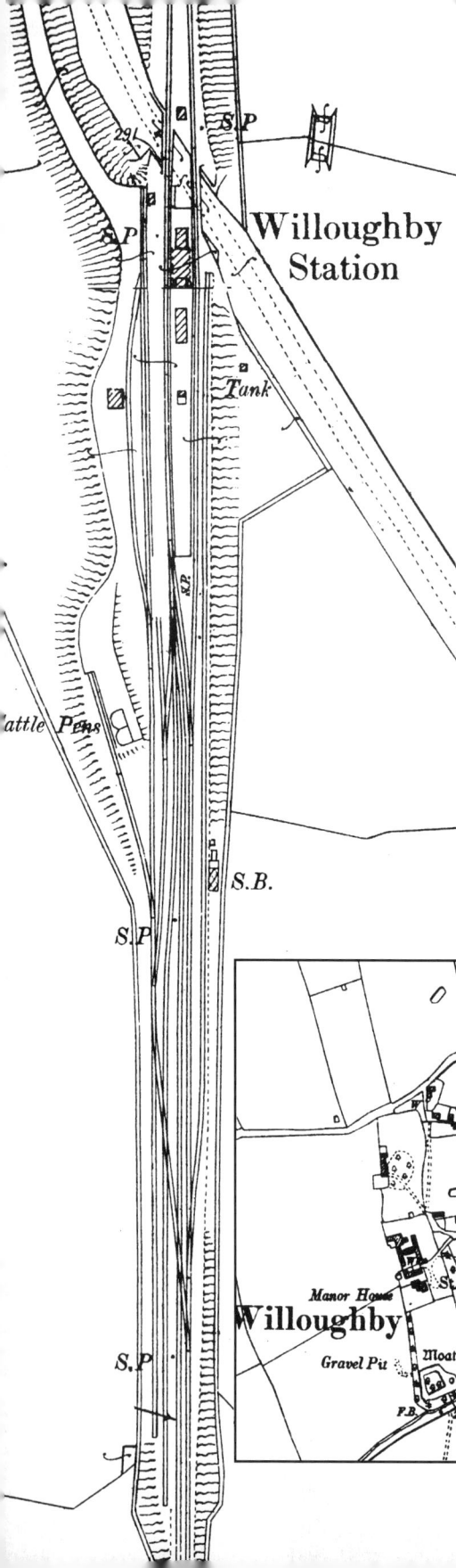

110.   The station water tank is in the background and in the foreground is the down refuge siding, which could accommodate 65 wagons. The ageing running-in board has a prop. (Stations UK)

XXX.   Inset is a six-inch scale map to indicate the close proximity of the village. Braunston returned a figure of 854 at the 1901 census, but Willoughby was only 279. The main map is from 1905, but the station name was Braunston; Willoughby was added on 1st January 1904.

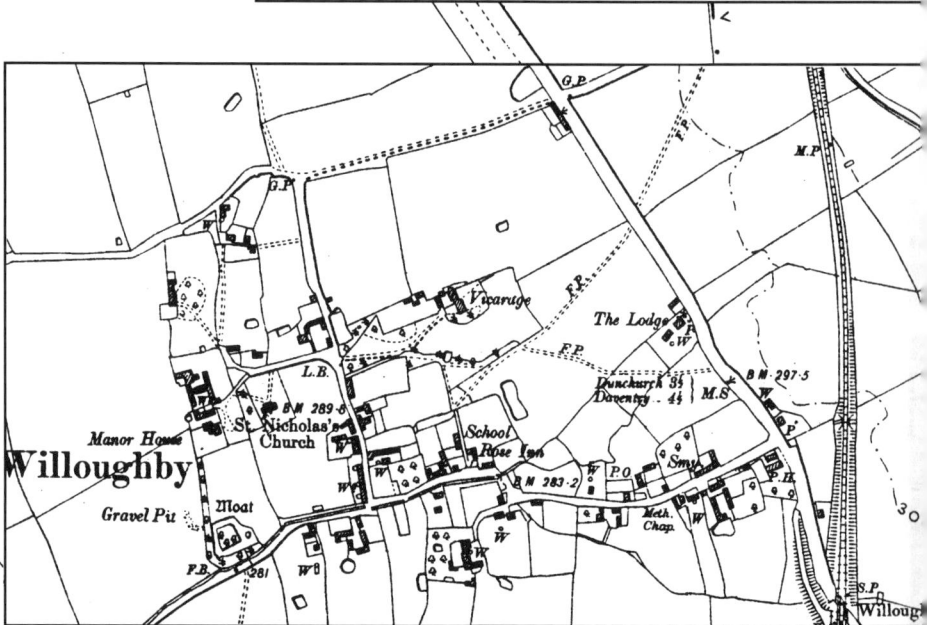

Willoughby Station

Tank

attle Pens

S.B.

S.P.

S.P.

Willoughby

Manor House

Gravel Pit

St Nicholas's Church

Vicarage

The Lodge

School

Rose Inn

Moat

111.   An ex-GCR class C 4-4-2 approaches with a down train in about 1935. The 40-lever signal box in the distance closed on 14th June 1965. Braunston had its own station on the LNWR from 1895, but it was not on a main line like this. (Stations UK)

112.   Freight and passenger services were withdrawn on 1st April 1957, a date misquoted in other volumes. This was earlier than the other 1899 stations on our journey. This is a shot from a passing train in about 1960. (D.C.Pearce coll.)

SOUTH OF RUGBY

113.   We are looking north on 25th June 1897 at the bridge carrying Dunchurch Road (now B4429), about one mile from the station. A further mile south was the location of Barby sidings which were laid out west of the main line in 1943 for the US Army. The 20-lever signal box closed on 29th September 1955, after the yard had been taken out of use. (R.M.Casserley coll.)

3rd-SINGLE   SINGLE-3rd

Braunston & Willoughby to

Braunston &	Braunston &
Willoughby	Willoughby
Rugby (Central)	Rugby (Central)

RUGBY (Central)

(M)   0/10   FARE   0/10   (M)

For conditions see over   For conditions see over

0176   0176

0063

B.T.C.   (M)
Bicycle Storage Ticket
The holder of this ticket is entitled to deposit a Bicycle at
Braunston & Willoughby
station for a period of SEVEN DAYS including date impressed on back hereof subject to the CONDITIONS ON BACK HEREOF.
This ticket must be produced for inspection when manded by a servant of the Commission.
Fee 1/0

B.T.C.   (M)
Bicycle Storage Ticket
Braunston & Willoughby
Valid for SEVEN DAYS including date impressed on back hereof.

0063

RUGBY CENTRAL

XXXI. The 1925 edition reveals that Hillmorton Road was widened to form a parking area at the station frontage. There is a refuge siding on the up side.

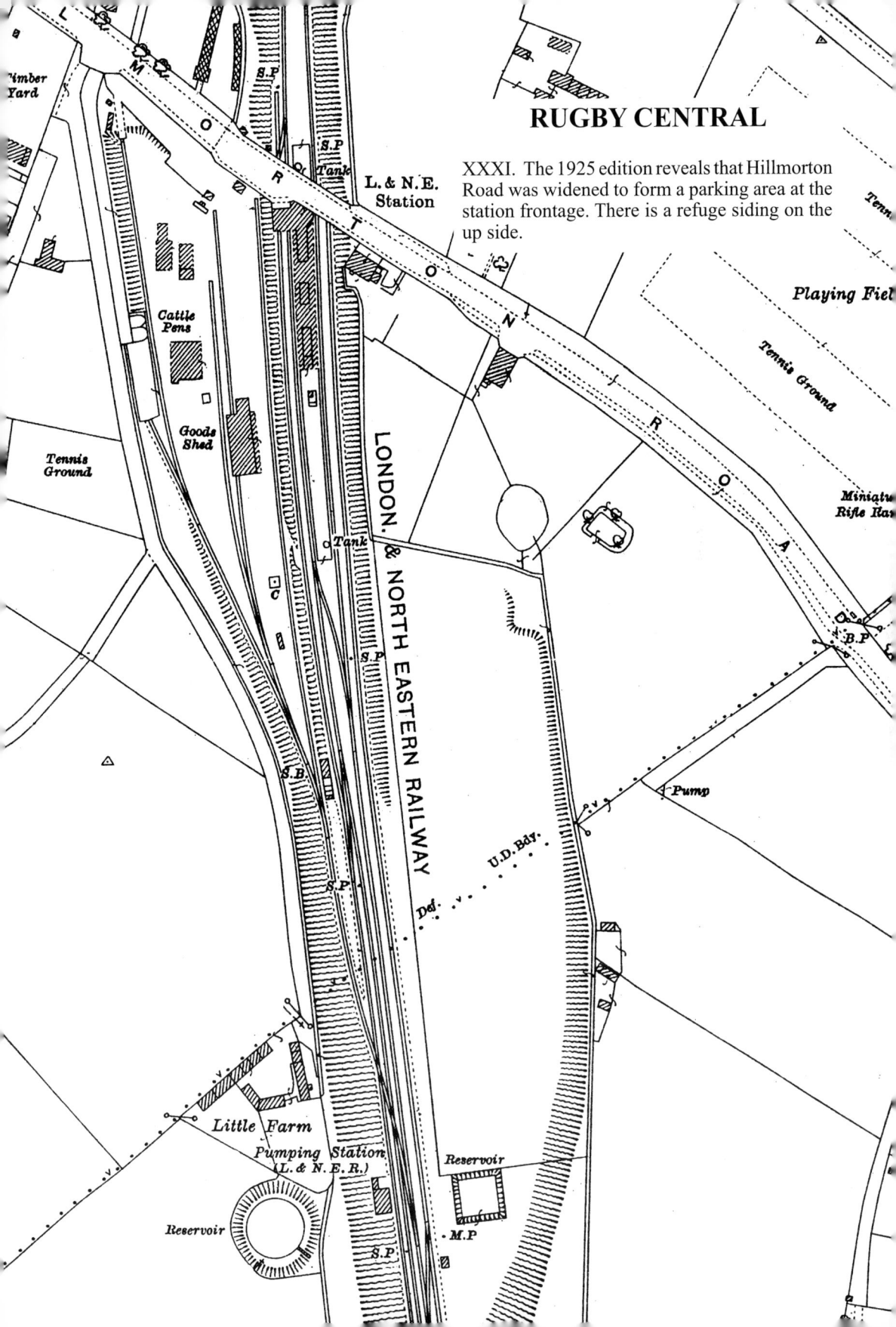

Timber Yard

S.P.

Tank

L. & N.E. Station

Playing Fiel

Tennis Ground

Cattle Pens

Goods Shed

Tennis Ground

Miniatu
Rifle Ran

S.B

Tank

C

LONDON & NORTH EASTERN RAILWAY

S.P.

Pump

S.B.

U.D.Bdy.

S.P.

Dd.

Little Farm
Pumping Station
(L. & N.E.R.)

Reservoir

Reservoir

M.P

S.P.

114.   Crowds gather round a down train in about 1910 as GCR class 8A 4-4-2 no. 192 waits to depart. The extension to the goods shed housed the office; its chimney is evident. (R.S.Carpenter coll.)

115.   The main line is on a gradient of 1 in 330 up towards the south, which explains the need for raised ground to create a level goods yard. A GCR 0-6-0 is shunting in about 1911. (R.S.Carpenter coll.)

116. The north elevation was recorded in 1951, with two Austin hire cars in attendance. The extremities of the structure spanned the tracks. (R.M.Casserley coll.)

L. N. E. R.
FURLOUGH
FOR CONDITIONS SEE BACK. Available for
three days, including day of issue.
RUGBY CENTRAL to
WENDOVER
Via Quainton Road
THIRD / Fur.Sing. \ CLASS
2158
WENDOVER

3991

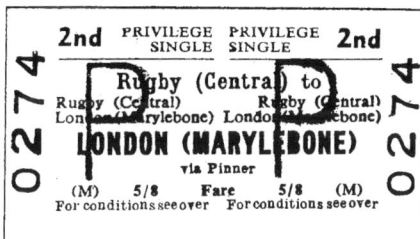

2nd PRIVILEGE PRIVILEGE 2nd
SINGLE SINGLE
Rugby (Central) to
Rugby (Central) Rugby (Central)
London (Marylebone) London (Marylebone)
LONDON (MARYLEBONE)
via Pinner
(M) 5/8 Fare 5/8 (M)
For conditions see over For conditions see over

0274

117.   The 10-ton crane is included in this August 1959 view of class B1 4-6-0 no. 61370 standing on the down refuge siding with an express. (A.W.V.Mace/Milepost 92½)

118.   "The South Yorkshireman" is passing through bound for Marylebone behind class B1 4-6-0 no. 61380, sometime in 1957. The headboard is too grimy to read easily. (A.W.V.Mace/Milepost 92½)

119.   The summit of the line in this area and the end of the up loop are in the distance. This loop had been formed from a refuge siding in 1941. The signal box (40 levers) remained in use until 5th May 1969, when the DMU service to Nottingham was withdrawn and the station closed completely. Class B16/3 4-6-0 no. 61444 is working back to York from Woodford in 1962. (D.C.Pearce coll.)

120.   The platform remained after closure and was later resurfaced as part of a public footpath. The goods shed (left) was incorporated into a timber yard. Freight traffic ceased on 14th June 1965 and staffing of the station came to an end on 5th September 1966, when all trains southwards were withdrawn. Class 5 4-6-0 no. 45277 races through with an up excursion in 1962. On the left, a local stopping train of compartment stock (plus two containers of meat) waits its turn to enter the platform. Some believe that the route, so well engineered by the GCR, may still have a future as a UK transport artery. (D.C.Pearce coll.)

MP Middleton Press

Easebourne Lane, Midhurst, West Sussex.
GU29 9AZ   Tel:01730 813169

EVOLVING THE ULTIMATE RAIL ENCYCLOPEDIA

www.middletonpress.co.uk   email:info@middletonpress.co.uk
A-0 906520   B-1 873793   C-1 901706   D-1 904474

OOP Out of print at time of printing - Please check availability   BROCHURE AVAILABLE SHOWING NEW TITLES